Sales Is a Relationship

Sales Is a Relationship

Lessons I've Learned in Business and Life

by
George Shea

with
Michael Brisciana

Copyright © 2025 by George Shea

ISBN: 979-8-9986905-4-9 (Paperback)
ISBN: 979-8-9986905-5-6 (Hardcover)

All rights reserved.

No part of this book may be reproduced or transmitted in any form whatsoever, including electronic or mechanical, photocopying, scanning, digitizing, recording, or captured by an informational storage or retrieval system without express written, dated, and signed permission from the author.

Brief excerpts from this book can be used for review purposes if the title and author of this book is cited and content is limited, as per accepted standards.

Published in the United States by Trust Publishing

Cover design by Michael Brisciana

Photographs courtesy of the author

DEDICATION

This book would not be possible without many important people in my life. There are way too many to mention and keep this short, but I also wanted to call out those who had the most direct connection to the stories in this book.

To my wife, Laura, and children, Laila and George: You are what inspires me every day of my life. I love you and thank you for making my life as great as it is.

To my dad: I miss you every day and am lucky to have spent the first 37 years of my life learning from you. I hope I can always share some of you through me, because you were too unbelievable to not be shared!

To my friends and family: Never has there ever been a better group of people to prop you up when you are down and bring you back to earth when you get a little too high! I am especially thankful to Anthony P., J.J. M., Mark M., Danielle M., Fran B., Bobby G., and Pauly D. You play very important roles in my life, and I greatly appreciate all of you.

To my "sales mentors": Dion G., Scott J, Rich S., Jim L., Blake H., Jimmy R., Tom F., Tony H., Hazen A., and many more. Thank you for teaching me the way to be a salesperson. I enjoyed every moment I was able to spend with you and am forever grateful.

There are hundreds more that deserve mention, but you will all have to wait until someone gets me to do a second book!

From the bottom of my heart: Thank you!

CONTENTS

Favorite Sales Quotations — 1

Introduction — 4

Author's Note — 6

SECTION 1: MY EARLY YEARS — 9

A 'Main Street USA' Childhood
My Mentor, My Dad
Adventures of the Road with Dad
Participating in Team and Individual Sports
Caddying Brought Many Benefits

Lesson 1: Being Comfortable in Social & Business Settings
Lesson 2: Making the Most of Opportunities
Lesson 3: Adapting to Your Environment
Lesson 4: Playing to Your Strengths
Lesson 5: Being Decent at Golf Doesn't Hurt Business
Lesson 6: Competing Sharpens Skills

Photographs From My Early Years

SECTION 2: MAKING MY WAY IN SALES — 28

Lesson 7: Taking Leaps of Faith
Lesson 8: Picking a Side (of the Organization)
Lesson 9: Know Who You Are and Act Accordingly
Lesson 10: You Haven't Earned It Until You've Earned It
Lesson 11: Learning From Great Mentors

Lesson 12: Thinking Outside the Box
Lesson 13: Diagnosing Problems and Helping People
Lesson 14: Having Humility
Lesson 15: You Have to Learn Some Lessons Again
Lesson 16: Learn Everything You Can About Your Profession
Lesson 17: Fitting the Approach to the Situation
Lesson 18: Keeping Your Career Exciting
Lesson 19: The Value of Persistence
Lesson 20: Presenting to Large and Small Groups
Lesson 21: Responding with Grace and Humor
Lesson 22: Going the Extra Mile (Literally)
Lesson 23: Managing Others and Managing Accounts
Lesson 24: Learning From Your Mentee
Lesson 25: Balancing Career and Family Isn't Easy
Lesson 26: Learning a New Industry

Mid-Career and Family Photographs

SECTION 3: LOOKING BACK AND FORWARD   72

Lesson 27: Stepping Outside Your Comfort Zone
Lesson 28: Having Courage to Go Out on Your Own
Lesson 29: What I've Learned from Starting My Own Firm
Lesson 30: Building the Right Culture for Your Team
Lesson 31: Bringing Others Along for Their Benefit
Lesson 32: Don't Swing Hard When a Soft Touch is Needed
Lesson 33: Don't Sell Past the Close
Lesson 34: Good Things Come with Self Discipline
Lesson 35: Learning to Read the Room
Lesson 36: Taking the Time to Get Leaders Comfortable
Lesson 37: Letting Someone Go as an Act of Kindness
Lesson 38: Maintaining Long-Term Relationships
Lesson 39: Build Trust by Solving Problems
Lesson 40: Being the One Who Cares the Most

Lesson 41: Using Humor to Good Effect
Lesson 42: Empathy Diffuses Anger
Lesson 43: Helping Leaders Help Themselves
Lesson 44: Keeping the Peace in Difficult Meetings
Lesson 45: Being the Same Person at All Times
Lesson 46: Due Diligence Builds Trust
Lesson 47: Spurring Out of the Box Thinking
Lesson 48: Negotiating Well Without Getting Greedy
Lesson 49: Doing Right and Setting an Example
Lesson 50: The Importance of Drive
Lesson 51: When They Count on You Personally
Lesson 52: Getting There (Planes and Automobiles)
Lesson 53: Always Pick Up the Tab
Lesson 54: Benefits of Marrying an Amazing Spouse
Lesson 55: Rooting for the Little Guy and Giving Back

Recent Customer and Family Photographs

About the Authors   131

About Shea Insurance Group   132

Favorite Quotes About Sales

As a "pre-introduction" or "warm-up" (like practice swings on the driving range before teeing off for a round of golf), I wanted to give you a flavor for the ideas and perspectives that I'll be sharing throughout this book. Below are a few favorite quotations about sales, business, and life. More are included at the beginning of each "lesson" or "tip." Enjoy!

❖ ❖ ❖ ❖ ❖ ❖ ❖

"To sell is to serve. Serve more, sell more."
Robin Sharma (Leadership Expert and Author, 2010s)

❖ ❖ ❖ ❖ ❖ ❖ ❖

"Don't sell life insurance. Sell what life insurance can do."
Ben Feldman (Legendary Life Insurance Salesman, 1960s)

❖ ❖ ❖ ❖ ❖ ❖ ❖

"Great salespeople are relationship builders who provide value and help their customers win."
Jeffrey Gitomer (Sales Expert and Author, 1990s)

❖ ❖ ❖ ❖ ❖ ❖ ❖

> *"The questions you ask are more important than the things you could ever say."*
> Thomas Freese (Author, *Question Based Selling*, 1999)

❖ ❖ ❖ ❖ ❖ ❖ ❖

> *"Success in sales comes from curiosity and caring, not charisma."*
> Deb Calvert (Sales Researcher and Trainer, 2010s)

❖ ❖ ❖ ❖ ❖ ❖ ❖

> *"The greatest salesperson in the world is one who sells with their heart as well as their head."*
> Og Mandino (Author, *The Greatest Salesman in the World*)

❖ ❖ ❖ ❖ ❖ ❖ ❖

> *"If you are going to persuade, you must first understand."*
> Aristotle (Greek Philosopher, circa 325 B.C.)

❖ ❖ ❖ ❖ ❖ ❖ ❖

> *"Selling is about making change happen. If you aren't helping the customer make a change, you're just collecting orders."*
> Jill Konrath (Sales Strategist and Author, 2010s)

❖ ❖ ❖ ❖ ❖ ❖ ❖

"Success is connected with action. Successful people keep moving. They make mistakes, but they don't quit."
Conrad Hilton (Founder of Hilton Hotels, 1950s)

❖   ❖   ❖   ❖   ❖   ❖   ❖

"The purpose of business is to create and keep a customer."
Peter Drucker (Management Consultant and Author, 1954)

INTRODUCTION

Hello, and welcome. My name is George Shea and I'm a salesman.

I'm also a father and husband; son, brother, and uncle; business owner and CEO; amateur golfer and youth sports coach; community member and neighbor; and friend and mentor.

I am fortunate to have had each of these roles during my life so far, and even more fortunate to have had wonderful mentors throughout my life. I wanted to write this book so that I could "give back" some of what I've been given by sharing some of the lessons that I've learned along the way. I hope that these humble thoughts, stories, memories and perspectives might help you in some way in your own personal or professional journeys.

To be candid, I've never aspired to be an author. While I'm not bad at putting my thoughts in writing and (mostly) knowing where the periods and commas go, at heart, I'm really more a "speaker" than a "writer," just based on personality and preference. While I've been told once or twice over the years that, "You must have a million stories – you should write a book," I never thought seriously about doing so until recently.

However, a few months ago, an author friend floated the idea of putting on paper the things that I've learned so far in business and in life. "I'll help," he said – and "it will be fun." Thankfully, he did more than help, and it truly has been a fun process. I have enjoyed walking down memory lane – recalling fond experiences from my past (some that I hadn't thought about in years) and trying to draw out common themes and "lessons" that might be useful to others.

Looking at these experiences altogether as I approach "middle age," what stands out to me the most is one simple thought. That is, sales – and life – is all about relationships.

The sales process is at its best, I believe, when it is a give-and-take, a sharing of ideas, a respectful exchange – between two people, or a group of people. When this is on-going, we call it a relationship. When relationships are at their best, they are about listening, understanding, and getting to know others, their passions, and their purposes. That is what I'm striving to accomplish when I'm "selling" – and it's what I'm trying to achieve in my personal relationships, as well. The better that I can relate to another human being, the better I can serve and support them. I believe that's what a life well-lived is all about.

Thank you for picking up this book today. It's so good to "meet" you and to begin our "relationship" in this way. I hope that these stories, perspective, and anecdotes will resonate and support you. It would be my great pleasure to serve you along the way!

George

George Shea
george@sheaig.com

Wayne, IL
November 2025

AUTHOR'S NOTES

To give you a "roadmap" to the book, I wanted to share a few notes upfront.

Writing Credits - Special thanks to Michael Brisciana for the idea of writing this book and offering his talents through hours of conversation to draw out these stories and ideas. His skill as an interviewer and writer has contributed mightily to the creation of this book.

Names and Places - With very limited exceptions, I've chosen not to include the names of companies or individuals in this book. I'm very grateful for all the friends, mentors, bosses, owners, colleagues, and team members who I've met along the way and who appear in the lessons, stories, and experiences described. However, I've kept them "anonymous" for two reasons:

1. To keep the focus on the general "lessons" of the stories shared, rather than the specific individuals and companies involved.

2. Out of respect for their privacy – particularly since I maintain ongoing personal and professional relationships with many of those mentioned.

To those who appear anonymously, I say in gratitude, "You know who you are" and how much you've done for me. Thank you, always!

Tone and Voice – While endeavoring to use proper grammar and punctuation, I've also tried hard to keep the text as "conversational" in tone and style as possible. Personally, I've always preferred the authentic over the prim and proper.

I hope that my "voice" comes through in the stories told and the lessons shared. As you're reading, picture if you will a voice with a happy tone and a face with a friendly grin. Most importantly, please don't blame my high school English teachers for any grammatical mistakes -- those are all on me!

Structure – For ease of use, the book is organized into three sections:

1. ***The Early Years*** – Formative experiences growing up in and around Chicago in the 1980's that shaped me for decades to come

2. ***Making My Way in the Sales World*** – Launching my career in sales out of town and on the road, learning my trade over two decades while working for two wonderful companies

3. ***Looking Back and Forward*** – Bringing us up to the present day, with later-career lessons, including the experience of starting my own firm and looking to the future.

Sales and Relationship Quotations – As you've already seen in the opening pages, I'm a big fan of quotations that say a lot in just a few words. Throughout each section I've included other famous (and not-so-famous) quotations about sales and life in general that apply to the tips and topics being discussed. A hat tip to ChatGPT for help identifying appropriate quotations and pithy sayings from sales gurus, political, business, sports, and spiritual leaders, and others with insights into sales and into life.

A Picture is Worth a Thousand Words – I have to admit that whenever I'm reading a non-fiction book like a biography or memoir, I turn right to the middle of the book to see if there are any pictures of the people or places mentioned. I'm guessing that most of us are the same in that way, looking for a "visual" to give us added context and information about the people involved.

If that describes you, too, I didn't want to disappoint! At the end of each section, you'll find a small collection of photographs of family, friends, and colleagues throughout the years. Many thanks to my family for assembling this collection.

SECTION 1:
MY EARLY YEARS

I was very fortunate to grow up in the American Midwest in the 1980's, where I got a little taste of both urban and suburban living. I was born in the city of Chicago on the northwest side of the city. It was a blue-collar, working-class neighborhood and we lived in a modest three-bedroom bungalow.

When I was born, I was the third child. Shortly after my arrival, another sibling came along, and finally one more several years later. While large families are less common today, at the time, having five children was nothing unusual for a typical Irish-Catholic family like ours. My mother's mother, my grandma, also lived with us in the bungalow.

I loved Chicago and – being from the north side -- I quickly and inevitably became a diehard Cubs fan, guided in my fandom by my grandma. Living near Wrigley Field, we were around the games all the time, which was always fun. As a youngster, I went to Cubs games with my grandma. As I got a little bit older, I would go to games with my buddies, which are memories that I cherish to this day.

A 'Main Street USA' Childhood

At seven or eight years old, we moved just west of the city because my parents were having their fifth child and wanted (and dearly needed) a larger house. We moved to the Near West suburbs, a little Italian neighborhood just outside of Chicago called Elmwood Park, where I lived until leaving for college.

Elmwood Park was a typical All-American suburb at that time – i.e., kids playing little league ball, families going to church on Sunday, 4th of July parades, and all of those types of things of happy memory. Similar to the neighborhood we had come from in the city, Elmwood Park was a working-class Italian area founded in the 1940's or 50s. By the time we got there in the 80s, it was a great, traditional place to grow up.

There's a big festival each summer that still goes on to this day, called The Taste of Elmwood Park, that was an annual highlight. There's a bunch of great restaurants in the area, and a lot of a local mom-and-pop joints from the neighboring areas all get together to showcase their wonderful food at "The Taste."

More than anything, what I remember the most is that it was a true neighborhood, where the local kids and families all knew each other. There were a million kids around, with tons of scheduled as well as pick-up games going on around you all the time across all the different seasons. You could jump on your bike (without a helmet in those days) and ride for two minutes and find a baseball or a football game somewhere – where you could play for the rest of the day without your parents worrying about where you were or who you were with.

I really feel lucky to have grown up in an environment like that. Looking back now, I'm sure that the sense of stability, neighborliness, safety, and comfort interacting with good people from all walks of life that my childhood offered shaped me in more ways that I realized – and continues to do so even now.

We're going to be talking a lot in this section of the book about how competing in sports shaped my career in so many ways. Before we do so, though, I feel the need to step back for a moment and share a few words about what (or really, who) was by far the biggest influence on my professional life – my dad.

My Mentor, My Dad

When I'm asked who my role models are, I have a pretty cheesy answer, but I'd be lying if I said anything different. There was one enormous role model in my life, and it was my dad -- George Shea "Senior" (or, just "George Shea," until I came along).

Back in the day, Dad was a sergeant in the U.S Army. After he got out of the army -- which he always jokingly said he joined because his mother's food was that bad, and he needed good cooking -- he was a lifelong salesman. When I was growing up, I don't think I realized what he did until I was probably close to my teenage years. Like most kids, I saw my dad go off to work and then come home, and I didn't think too much about the time in-between. However, thinking about it now, just watching him deal with people had an enormous impact on me and my siblings.

It's a corny thing to say, I know, but Dad truly had an ability to light up a room. I never saw him look uncomfortable in any situation, whether it was a barbecue, a family party, a business meeting, or a tense situation where maybe tempers were starting to flair. It was amazing to me that somebody was always so comfortable in their own skin and knew exactly how to deal with situations – often with gentle humor or finding a way to "lower the temperature" and help everyone get the most out of encounter.

For these and many other reasons, he'll always be my mentor.

Adventures on the Road with Dad

To give you a snippet of what this looked like in real life, I have a favorite memory of Dad from childhood. When we were on summer break from school, being that there were five of us kids (which was a lot to contend with for my mom, as we were a "spirited" bunch), Dad used to do my mom a favor and take one of us on some of his business trips.

At that time in his career, Dad was a senior salesperson for a large industrial company. He had worked his way up to where the territories he was responsible for spanned across the whole country. This meant a lot of driving in whatever region he was focusing on that particular week. So, if he was going from Chicago to Michigan or Wisconsin or Minnesota, for example, a lot of times, he would take one of the kids with him. This is how I got to see him in action in boardrooms, shop floors, and even lunches or dinners with customers.

Back in the late 80s and 90s, most customers didn't mind if people brought along their kids, as long as we were well-behaved (we wouldn't dare act up!) and weren't getting in the way of business. It was cool to see him "do his thing" in these settings, and I think that also helped add several layers of confidence for me and how I deal with people.

A little later in the book, I'll get back to how this influenced me from a "sales" perspective. For right now, though, I wanted to mention those trips, as they are some of my fondest memories from my childhood. Being from a large family, there wasn't a lot of one-on-one time with your parents. Getting that time – in whatever form it took -- was always special. We didn't travel "fancy" – just decent motels or hotels and eating at local diners and roadside restaurants. For me-- like the old Mastercard commercials used to say – having an adventure on the road with my dad was "priceless."

Participating in Team and Individual Sports

I'll have a lot more sales-related stories to share about my dad later in the book. For the moment, though, I want to get back to other influences during my growing-up years – namely, sports.

I have enjoyed participating in sports my whole life – both playing and watching. I believe that lessons learned from competing in sports – from training to strategizing, and from learning to adapt to changing conditions to learning how to win and lose with grace – influence me to this day.

Football and baseball were my favorites growing up – later adding golf in high school, college, and adulthood. As a kid, I played a range of different sports, depending on the season and if any minor injuries were limiting me at the time. I always enjoyed team sports because you're relying not just on yourself, but on several other people to do the right thing at the right time for things to go well. Trusting in your teammates turned out to be a very good life lesson. It takes a lot of practice – and having confidence in each other to do your own "jobs" – for the team to excel.

I got a chance to play a lot of organized baseball and football as a youngster. In junior high school, I even got a chance to play soccer and basketball, which I enjoyed, as well – I was just a very sports-focused kid. I wasn't good enough at baseball to play in high school, which is when I started getting into golf. This was a "happy accident" in many ways, as it opened me up to a wide range of new experiences (more about that, later).

Switching over to golf was particularly interesting to me because it was really the first solo sport that I had ever played. I found that golf teaches you a different life lesson because you're not relying on a team. At that point, you're relying on yourself and your own set of skills. I found that this taught me how to be mentally strong, and how to adapt.

You have to be able to think on your feet and make quick adaptations – like changing the way you're attacking an opponent or the strategy that you're using. I'll say more about the "adapting quickly" idea, below.

Becoming a Caddy Brought Many Benefits

I don't think that I realized this as it was happening, but so many of the biggest influences on me (other than my family) have revolved around golf. My experiences on and around the course exposed me to many different influences than I had in school or at home. I'm very grateful for how these interactions caused me to expand my horizons and brought me in contact with people, ideas, and perspectives that continue to influence and benefit me to this day.

I started caddying when I was 12 years old. It happened that there was a country club about five minutes away from where we lived after we moved out to the suburbs in Elmwood Park. While my friends would generally cut lawns or worked at fast food places during summer breaks in high school, I was very fortunate to be in the right place at the right time and ended up with a job caddying at a local golf course.

The way this got started was, one day one of my friends who worked at the course let me know that they needed extra help. I guess I must have done a decent job that first day, so they kept inviting me back – and the rest, as they say, is history. During my high school and college years, this was my main way of earning pocket money.

One of the many lessons caddying taught me was how to be a better conversationalist. By personality, I'm a naturally "chatty" person – so, being comfortable interacting with people is part of my nature. My golf-related experiences served to enhance whatever natural tendencies I may have had in this area. This leads to the first "lesson" (or "tip" or "pointer") that I would like to share with you.

"People buy from people they trust and like."
John C. Maxwell (Leadership Expert, 1990s)

LESSON 1:
Being Comfortable in Social & Business Settings

For those who might not be familiar with golf, when you're caddying, you're carrying the bags for players on the course -- estimating distances to the hole, suggesting a club for them to use on a particular shot, and helping them navigate the course successfully. Since you're out on the course together for anywhere from two to five hours – most of which is spent waiting for others to play their shots – there's a lot of time for casual conversation. That's the part that really impacted me.

Given that golf is largely a "country club" type of sport, you're often dealing with CEO or "C-level" executives or other people of a certain stature or level of accomplishment in these clubs, whether they're members or invited guests. I found that interacting with people like this taught me how to be part of respectful conversations, how to make gracious introductions, when to offer to buy a round of drinks, etc. -- among other important social cues and niceties.

Seeing how these executives and community leaders engaged with others was extremely interesting to me. I tried to soak it all, taking "mental notes" about those who seemed to thrive in these situations, and absorbing as much as I could of what was then a new world for me.

There were several different skills and "lessons" that I took in through these experiences.

1 – Being comfortable in different "levels" of society

I was a middle-class kid and didn't grow up in a country club type of family. Then by the time I was in my early 20s, I was spending a lot of time at country clubs – first caddying, and then once I began my sales career, playing with clients and prospects. I believe that this exposure made me more comfortable being in a variety of social and business situations and interacting with a wide range of people in different segments of society.

To put it differently, while I'm a "beer and brats in the backyard" kind of guy at heart, it helps to be comfortable in other environments – from "champagne and caviar" receptions and "black tie" fundraising events, to "Taco Tuesday" at the food truck down the street, and everything in-between. I've found many of my best prospects and friends in all these places.

2 – Being good at "small talk" and making others comfortable around you

Even for the most extroverted among us, new social situations can make people nervous. One thing I learned caddying is how the most successful (and beloved) executives had a knack for "small talk" that was anything but small. That is, while chatting about family, sports, and other topics of general interest, they had a way of getting people to relax and interact freely without having to worry about saying the wrong thing or embarrassing themselves in new situations. For this reason, people tended to gravitate toward them and good and true relationships would develop. (Who wouldn't want to spend time around someone who makes you feel good just by being in their presence?).

For some people (like my dad), this is a natural ability. For others, it's more of a learned behavior. Either way, it struck me as a very important skill to have in any situation, from business to social – and I've tried to improve my ability to make others comfortable every chance I have. There's no downside to treating others with respect and having people like you!

❖ ❖ ❖ ❖ ❖ ❖ ❖

"Regrets, I've had a few, but too few to mention."
Frank Sinatra (American singer - My Way, circa 1974)

LESSON 2:
Making the Most of Opportunities

The impact that golf has had on me got stronger when I had a chance to play at a collegiate level -- starting at a small school in Iowa and then transferring to an in-state school in southern Illinois. This brought with it so many good things – and one "regret," as well.

I don't have many regrets in life, as I try to learn from every experience and move on to the next. To be candid, though, I'd love to go back and redo those days and take my college golf career a lot more seriously. I think that I could have gone further than I did – and even if that wasn't the case, I could have challenged myself more rigorously.

Like many a college student, though, the lures of burgeoning social opportunities (and perhaps a pint or two of beer) sometimes proved more powerful than the desire to practice my swing night and day. I guess you can say I was "practicing my social skills" at this time – but I'm sure that I could have done that and still worked on my golf skills at an even higher level of intensity and focus.

Even so, it was quite an experience to have the chance to play sports in college. It was an extremely neat way to make great friends, bond with teammates, and to learn about golf and about life from wise coaches. We had a great time together – from long bus rides, to competing together, to just "shooting the breeze" late in the evening.

While I miss those days, I'm very thankful for the opportunities competing in collegiate golf have brought to me. Now, like most parents, I'm left to live vicariously through my children's athletic pursuits (no pressure, kids!) – which (no kidding, now) is a great joy in my life.

Continuing with our golfing theme, I wanted to share with you other "lessons learned" on the course and in the clubhouse.

❖   ❖   ❖   ❖   ❖   ❖   ❖

"The pessimist complains about the wind; the optimist expects it to change; the realist adjusts the sails."
William Arthur Ward (Motivational writer, 1921 – 1994)

LESSON 3:
Adapting to Your Environment

One of the many life lessons I learned from golf is the importance of paying attention to your environment and preparing and adapting accordingly. As an example of this, let's consider something as commonplace as the changing weather.

From time to time, like all golfers, I'm guilty of not checking the weather ahead of time and finding myself in the middle of the fairway without an umbrella as a (predicted) torrential downfall besieges us. On the surface, this is a lesson to follow the old Boy Scout's Credo to "Always Be Prepared." That part is obvious, of course. The slightly more nuanced "tip" that I wanted to share here, though, has to do with adapting to conditions as they change.

You can think that you're prepared for anything – but if you can't adapt on the fly, then your preparations will often be for naught.

For example, let's say that you start your Saturday afternoon round of golf when it's 72 degrees, sunny, and dry. Under these conditions, the course will play one way (usually a lot "faster") and you'll need to use certain clubs and strategies.

However, let's say that the winds shift, a front moves in, and over the course of an hour or two, the temperature drops by 15 degrees (which isn't unusual in the Mid-West!), and a cold drizzle begins to come down. Under these new conditions, the course is likely to play very differently than when you began your round – and a different approach will be needed. You have to be ready for anything and then adapt accordingly.

In business, this might translate into "reading the room" – i.e., knowing who is in the meeting and what the collective "mood" is -- and adapting your presentation accordingly. Knowing if you have a friendly crowd or a hostile audience – and being able to alter your approach in either direction – can often spell the difference between success or failure in a meeting.

Let's say that you're giving an "Open Enrollment" presentation about your client's new health benefits plans to different groups of employees throughout the day. You might have had a friendly audience in the first presentation of the day, and a hostile crowd in the second meeting. If you try to use the same approach in the second meeting as you used in the first, it's probably not going to go very well. Staying alert to your environment and being able to adapt is key to success.

If you've only prepared one "spiel" and don't have the materials, confidence, or command of your content to take a different course mid-stream, you may find yourself unexpectedly playing to a "rough crowd" with no way to improve the situation. If, however, you can pull an "alternative pitch" out of your back pocket – or, depending on the level of emotion involved, if you decide to throw out the script entirely and "ad lib" the presentation based on the needs and concerns of the group in front of you – you're much more likely to come out of the meeting successfully. At the very least, you will have succeeded in building a trusting relationship with your audience – showing them that you're taking their concerns seriously, rather than just "jamming a script down their throats," regardless of whether it meets their immediate needs and worries.

To borrow a metaphor from another sport: As the great boxer Mike Tyson once said, "Everybody has a great plan until you get punched in the mouth." You've got to be able to make changes to what your game plan was, based on the reality of the situation at that moment.

"Knowing yourself is the beginning of all wisdom."
Aristotle (philosopher, Ancient Greece)

LESSON 4:
Playing to Your Strengths

Another lesson that I learned from playing golf (and sports, in general) is the need to recognize your and your opponent's relative strengths and weaknesses, and to plan accordingly. It's important to consider what they do best. Are they strong, mentally (i.e., are they at their best under pressure, or do they get nervous when approaching the big shots)? Are they strong physically in their game (i.e., can they make shots from all over the golf course – or do they struggle with one type of shot or another)?

Let's say you're playing someone who can hit the ball 50 yards further than you (which, in most cases is a huge advantage in golf). You've got to make a quick decision. Am I going to try to swing out of my shoes and keep up with them (which I probably can't succeed at, even if I try)? Or am I going to try to play my own game and score that way -- which is generally the smartest way to go. If you're not capable of hitting long bombs off the tee but you try to do so anyway, you can get yourself in a lot of trouble very quickly. You need to be self-aware of what you're good at and what you're not good at.

Let's translate this to a sales situation. Let's say that you know that your competitor has a very strong marketing department that provides them with very sleek-looking videos and collateral material. By contrast, you're just starting out and the only "leave behind" you have at this point is a one-page Word document that you printed out on your portable printer in the hotel the night before. You could choose to stay up all night working on the fanciest presentation that you can come up with – but you know graphics and technology aren't your strong suits.

You're probably much better off doubling down on your strengths – i.e., putting all your energy into developing a positive rapport with the client based on a desire to help them – rather than competing on a field that plays to your competitor's strengths where you're unlikely to win.

The more areas you can get your skills up to at least an acceptable level, the better you'll be able to compete. However, you're most likely to come out on top – in sports, in sales, and in life – if you have self-awareness and focus on maximizing your strengths and minimizing your weaknesses on the course or in the meeting room.

"A good golfer has the determination to win and the patience to wait for the breaks."
Gary Player (Hall of Fame PGA golfer, South Africa)

LESSON 5:
Being Decent at Golf Doesn't Hurt Business

As I said at the beginning of the book, I've been fortunate in many aspects of my life. One such lucky break that helped me was being reasonably good at golf. Granted, this was much more true in my younger, more athletic days, of course. However, even now – at my more "advanced" age – being able to host a round of golf for clients or prospects is always a joy, and an aid to business.

If you're lucky enough to be a single digit handicap (which is a good level compared to most others) and you go out there with a bunch of "weekend warriors" that just want to have a fun day on the course, they naturally gravitate towards you because it's something where you're excelling. You don't even have to be that good – as long as you can navigate your way around the course without losing too many balls or holding up your foursome too often, it makes for a relaxing time getting to know clients and building the relationship.

The combination of being comfortable on the course and being good at the game, I think was, was very beneficial to me, helping me carrying myself with a little additional confidence out there. The same comfort and confidence can carry over to sales meetings, presentations, or other life endeavors. When a customer or prospect jumps at your invitation to play a round together, it's never a bad thing. Even if they accept your invitation because they just want to play a certain course and they're not really interested in your product or service, having several hours of one-on-one time on the course together is always to your benefit.

At those times where "business" isn't discussed directly on the course – or when it's touched on just briefly while having a celebratory drink at the "19th Hole" afterward – you're still developing the relationship and building trust and rapport, no matter what. It may not result in an immediate sale, of course – but if I'm in an ongoing conversation or relationship with someone, I feel like I've always "got a shot" (pardon the pun) in the future.

Before wrapping up this section on my early years, there is one more family and sports-related "lesson" that I wanted to share.

❖   ❖   ❖   ❖   ❖   ❖   ❖

"A horse never runs so fast as when he has other horses to catch up and outpace."
Ovid (poet, Ancient Rome, 43 BC – 17 AD)

LESSON 6:
Competing Sharpens Skills

To succeed in sales, having some measure of a competitive spirit is absolutely required, I believe. Being competitive is part of my nature, as well as my brother and other family members. If I go back to my childhood days, whether it was playing Scrabble on a long winter's night, or fishing on the lake in summer, or other games we would make up with neighborhood kids, I was always naturally pretty competitive. In my family – up to and including my grandma who lived with us – you weren't giving out up any wins -- you wanted to win the game.

It is said that competition can bring out the best and worst in people. In my experience, it is most often "the best" rather than "the worst" – as long as it is not taken to extremes, of course (i.e., no cheating, lying, taking unfair advantage, etc.). I've found that it helps keep you "on your toes" and stretching to be better than you may have thought you could be. This is good and healthy in many ways in sales, where it pays to remember the adage that "If you're not taking care of your customers, someone else will" – i.e., there's no time for resting on laurels or putting in half-hearted efforts. You're always competing with someone, whether you know it or not.

I've always enjoyed healthy competition with my brother, who also made his career in sales. We have often worked in similar industries, so there's always been lots of room for comparison between us – though, he's probably much nicer and kinder than I am. (Please don't tell him I said that, as I need to maintain my younger-brother edge).

I always thought it would be cool to work along with him in some regard – but we never have done so, up until now. (You never know what the future might hold, of course). I don't want to say it makes me sad, but maybe "wistful" is the word. Then again, maybe it's good that we haven't worked together since it might have brought out the uber competitive side of both of us – which wouldn't necessarily make for a positive family dynamic at Thanksgiving dinner.

It was sure a heck of a lot of fun back then, though.

I miss those days!

PHOTOS FROM MY EARLY YEARS

Christmastime fun with my dad and younger sister.

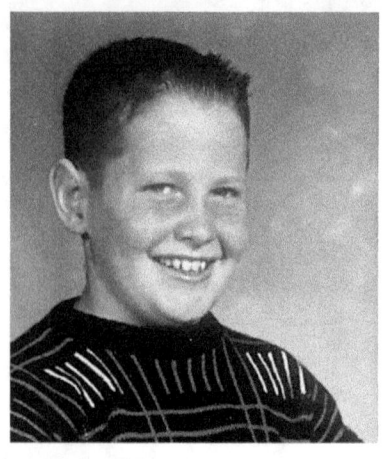

Middle school photo during my "sweater" period

Summertime clowning around with my brother and older sister

Family camping trip with my brother

Dinner with my mom during my high school years

Out at the neighborhood bar with friends

SECTION 2:
MAKING MY WAY IN SALES

With my happy childhood behind me, I was eager to get my start in the world after my college days. Looking up to my dad the way that I did, I always wanted to be in same field as him. I'm not sure that I made a conscious decision about this – but selling always looked like fun to me (at least, the way Dad did it). I'm so glad and grateful to be able to say that it is still fun for me almost 30 years later.

In this section, I want to share some experiences and lessons from early in my professional career. From having great mentors, to being given the chance to develop my skills on the road on my own, my early years working as a sales representative brought many lessons – along with fond memories of the people who helped me along the way.

Starting My Sales Career in Kansas City

I was actually hired into my first sales job by someone who had previously worked for my dad. Dad was working in a different division of a large, industrial company at that time. Because there was no interaction between our divisions or individual roles, there wasn't any problem with "conflict of interest" or "anti-nepotism" rules.

I write about that company a lot throughout this book because it was a terrific experience that taught me what it meant to be a sales professional. I learned so much watching great salespeople there, to whom – in addition to my dad – I owe so much of my later career success.

It's funny how things work out, sometimes. Growing up, whenever dad brought us around to his office, there was a guy who always said that he wanted to hire me or my brother, or both of us, when we finished school. It's funny how things work out sometimes, as people often say things like that but they rarely come to fruition. In this case, though, he ended up making me an offer and I was thrilled to accept it without a second thought.

I was on my way! I wasn't sure exactly what I was on my way to – but it was a start, and that's all that mattered. Somewhere in the back of my mind, I knew that I'd get great experience and maybe even have an adventure or two along the way. I got the job and then -- right off the bat -- I was told that I was moving from Chicago to Kansas City and I would be covering four states in the region. As far as I was concerned, it was full speed ahead!

❖   ❖   ❖   ❖   ❖   ❖   ❖

"A ship is safe in harbor, but that's not what ships are built for."
John A. Shedd (Author, Salt from My Attic, 1928)

LESSON 7:
Taking Leaps of Faith

One of the main lessons that I learned from this time in my life is the importance of taking "leaps of faith" to get to where you're going. Leaving the friendly confines of my family and the only life I had ever known in Chicago and venturing out to Kansas City was one such leap. It ended up being an excellent experience both professionally and personally (in terms of growing and maturing) – and one that I've never regretted.

Moving out to Kansas City was the first time -- other than college -- where I was out on my own. It felt like it happened very quickly -- school was done and the next thing I knew, I was out on the road selling. I think it helped me that I had to dive in so quickly, as I didn't have time to get nervous or worried or anything like that. I was just charged up and ready to take on the world – or, at least, my little corner of it – to prove my worth, and to make my dad (and myself) proud.

My first task was to get acclimated to my new city: Kansas City. After staying in a hotel in my first few weeks there, I made it my mission to find a permanent place to live. After that, my goal was to find my way around town and around my region.

This was in the early 2000's. Cellphones were still relatively new devices and smartphones and apps weren't a thing yet – neither was Google Maps. GPSs in cars were brand new devices that almost nobody had because they were expensive. It was still mostly an "analog" and "paper" world at that time. So, I headed to the AAA office and picked up four states worth of road maps. I had to drive to see customers across the region and maps and handwritten directions were the only way to navigate.

It was neat to know that I was on my own, but it was also scary having that big of an area as my first sales territory. In a way, I really had to "learn" the ins and outs of several states, rather than just one new city. Being a Midwesterner at heart, it didn't seem all that hard – but you never know until you do it, right? In any case, after a few months, everything settled in and I felt well-acclimated.

The kind of nervous excitement that I felt in those early days, I think, is helpful in sales because it makes you want to be successful. You don't admit it to anyone, but you're secretly afraid of doing a bad job and getting fired and being sent home with your tail between your legs. A little fear of failure isn't a bad thing – as long as it doesn't overwhelm you.

All these years later, my main take-away is that if I hadn't taken that "leap of faith" – if I had been wedded to the idea of "Chicago, and Chicago Only" for my first job – there's no telling how differently my career and life may have proceeded.

I'm very happy that report, though, that I did take that "leap" and survived to tell the tale. So, with apologies to the late great radio raconteur, Paul Harvey, here is "the rest of the story" (or, at least, the next part of the story).

"Nothing happens until someone sells something."
Henry Ford (Founder, Ford Motor Company, 1920s)

LESSON 8:
Picking a Side (of the Organization)

In most organizations, there's always a subtle (and sometimes, not so subtle) tension between the engineering side of the company that focuses on the particulars of the product and the sales side, whose utmost concern is making the sale, booking the revenue (and commission), and moving on to the next potential customer. For example, an engineer might alter the quote above to read, "Nothing happens until someone makes something" (which is also true, of course).

There's nothing wrong with this tension, per se – as long as it doesn't harden into animosities or bitter rivalries in the organization. In my experience, it's best when both sides work together as a team, with each bringing their expertise to the table in a respectful way, for the good of the customer and of the company.

Usually, most people end up on one side (engineering, operations, etc.) or the other (sales, account management, etc.), depending on their talents, interests, and drive. This isn't to discount or ignore the other functions of an organization (i.e., Accounting, Human Resources, I.T., etc.). It's just that those functions – all of which are critical players in the organization's overall success – by their nature generally attract individuals with different personality profiles than Operations or Sales. In any case, back to "the choice."

By this point in the book, I'm sure that you won't be surprised to hear me admit that I'm a sales guy, through and through. I don't want to take away from the importance of the product -- because if you don't have a quality product, then you have nothing to sell. But it is the sales part of the process that excites me the most.

The point here is that you have to be "true to yourself" and your passions – and hopefully, you'll be lucky enough to find a job (or create one) that aligns with both your skills and your passions. Fortunately, for me, I've always been friends with both "sides."

Starting out in the industrial company, I was a salesperson – so, I spent most of my time with other salespeople. At the same time, it was important to understand the products as in-depth as I could, which caused me to also spend a lot of time with the engineers. All of this led me to the belief that a company can't truly be great unless both groups are operating at the top of their game and working well together. As they say, "Teamwork makes the dream work." (But I'm still a sales guy!).

❖   ❖   ❖   ❖   ❖   ❖   ❖

"Be yourself; everyone else is already taken."
Oscar Wilde (Irish playwright and wit, circa 1890s)

LESSON 9:
Know Who You Are and Act Accordingly

While we've talked about "sales" in general thus far, it's worth taking a moment or two to share a few thoughts about the different types of salespeople that are out there. I think it helpful to recognize which "type" is closest to your natural style – and then to focus your efforts accordingly. Knowing where your preference and skills lay will save you a great deal of time and anxiety by avoiding being in a role that isn't a good fit for you.

One of the simplest ways to think about this is to consider "hunters" and "farmers." Hunters are generally drawn to the "kill" (i.e., closing sales), whereas farmers tend to focus more on maintaining accounts once the customer is onboard. Hunters tend to be more eager to pursue new opportunities, close deals, and then move on to the next opportunity. Farmers tend to focus more on cultivating existing relationships so that recurring sales to these customers grow from year to year, guaranteeing steady and predictable income.

To really excel in sales, I think you have to be adequate at one of them and great at the other one, but you need to be at least good at both.

Even if you are a hunter, you must know how to support customers. Otherwise, you're going to end up losing that account eventually. If servicing customers is boring for you, the customer is going to feel the lack of warmth and you're going to lose them, sooner or later.

Overall, I think more salespeople have a natural tendency toward account management. It's a more comfortable role because you're not constantly pushing people to sign on the dotted line (and to do so now). A good account manager is still "money-focused" – it's just that by nature, they believe the best route to growing accounts is to service (some say "delight") customers, cementing the relationship and leading to higher sales.

My Preference -- For myself, I enjoy the thrill of the hunt, which is the most fun part of sales for me. I love finding and bringing on new customers. What I love even more is when I can actually solve a problem for somebody through our products or services. This isn't a sales thing. It is just a human thing.

Most good salespeople (both hunters and farmers) are "pleasers." They want to please the customer, because that gives them a good feeling on the inside. When all is said and done, that's always been the most fun part for me.

In Praise of Hunters -- To say one final thing about hunters, it's that when you see a good one, they are fun to behold. I know many of them and I'm a huge fan. They are just "all in" and totally focused on doing everything and anything they need to do to get the sale (within the realm of ethics, of course).

Like everything else in life, though, balance is needed. When a hunter has no interest in account management, this often leads to a high turnover rate with their customer base -- unless they're lucky enough to have a great account management team around them to pick up the slack. If they don't have a great support team, it's like watching a slow-motion plane crash in progress – you know they're going to lose client sooner rather than later. We try to avoid crashes at all costs, of course.

❖   ❖   ❖   ❖   ❖   ❖   ❖

"Humility is not thinking less of yourself, it's thinking of yourself less."
C.S. Lewis (Author and theologian, *Mere Christianity*)

LESSON 10:
You Haven't Earned It Until You've Earned It

Early on in that first job, I had to visit the corporate offices, which were out on the East Coast. As was his custom, the owner of the company very kindly stopped by to visit me and other new recruits while I was there. It was an honor just to have him take the time to seek me out (aided, I'm sure, by the fact that my dad was a well-respected man within the company).

Remember that I was 23 years old at this point -- young and naïve and maybe even a slight bit cocky (I'd like to leave it at "confident," but "cocky" is probably a little closer to the truth). While I had heard a lot about the owner through my dad and others, I had never met him face to face. They brought me into the boardroom to meet him, and a couple of the higher-ups were there with him.

The gentleman that he was, the owner greeted me with a warm smile and a handshake, saying "It's good to have another George Shea on board." (My dad's name is also George Shea).

Trying to portray my confidence, confidence, and energy to him all in one fell swoop, I said with enthusiasm, "Yeah,

I'm just a replica of my dad," giving myself unearned credit, of course.

Not missing a beat, the owner responded, "Oh, we'll find out real quick if you're a replica, or if you're a cheap copy."

While he said it with a wink and a smile, his point was clear and well-made. It took me down a peg or two, to say the least.

He was right to say it, of course – as painful as it might have been to hear at that moment. I'm sure that I had gone in there a little bit too confident in myself. The owner saw this right away and let me know in his own way, "You've got the 'name,' kid, but let's see what you can do out there." He was taking a page from the great NFL Coach, Bill Parcells, who once remarked about a "star" rookie, "Let's not measure him for a Hall of Fame jacket quite yet!"

The lesson here is that none of us has "earned" anything until we've earned it. A "name" might get you in the door, but it won't keep you there. You have to earn your place every day. It's something that I've never forgotten all these years later, and it inspired me to prove that I could hold my own.

As I reflect on that early comparison to my dad, I don't think I'll ever be nearly the salesperson my dad was, because he was the best I've ever seen. It's fun to know, though, that I've been at least moderately successful in the same field as Dad – and that I've been able to show people that I could do a good job. I might not always do it the same way that he did, but I've worked hard and am proud to honor his legacy in some small way with my own successes.

None of this would have been possible without him and everyone else who guided me along the way.

❖ ❖ ❖ ❖ ❖ ❖ ❖

"Mentoring is a brain to pick, an ear to listen, and a push in the right direction."
John C. Crosby (American politician, 1910s)

LESSON 11:
Learning from Great Mentors

I'm often asked how I "learned" sales, particularly in my first sales job with the industrial company. The short answer is that I learned the business by spending time with people on the Operations side of the house – and I learned Sales from informal (but very effective) mentoring from senior salespeople at the company. Here's a little background on how that came to be.

Starting out with the industrial company, I spent a few weeks in the warehouse seeing the guys pick the orders, getting to know the parts, talking with different departments, and seeking out product managers to learn about specific products.

After that, the main part of my Sales education early on came from long drives with experienced salespeople that knew the industry and the customers very well. I would watch them closely – observing how they ran a customer meeting, how they used samples, how they explained the products, how they asked questions, how they listened to the answers, and then how they replied with thoughtful follow-up questions and answers.

I tell people all the time that I learned the most about sales in those early years. I don't like throwing around the word "blessed," but I was blessed to be with that crew of sales guys, learning how they did things and seeing different styles. It exposed me to so many different approaches, so that I could then pick and choose what styles and approaches worked best for me.

If there's one talent that I think I have, I would say that it's watching what someone is doing, picking apart what's working and what's not working, and then incorporating the good parts into my own practices. Seeing those seasoned veterans go to battle on a day-to-day basis and getting to know how they approach things was an invaluable learning experience in this way.

There was a lot of "coaching and mentoring" going on in those conversations in a very subtle way. That term wasn't in our vocabularies in those days and probably would have been dismissed out of hand if it was mentioned – however, it was coaching and mentoring, nevertheless.

One way that I mean this is that it's always a good thing to have someone looking out for you, warning you against touching the hot stove so that you don't have to burn yourself. This was rarely direct in terms of being told, "Do this. Don't do that" – but you could always read between the lines when they were telling you really not to do something. Mostly, though, it was teaching by example – and I loved and benefited from every minute of it.

Long drives and quick feedback - In my first territory working for that company, I was covering four states -- Iowa, Missouri, Nebraska, and Kansas. It's not like I was in Chicago or in New York where you can walk from one meeting to another a block away in just a few minutes. Rather, there would be an hour and a half or two hour drives in between some of these meetings, so you had a lot of time for good talks with the mentor sitting in the driver's seat, if you chose to use the time wisely.

I think that was very helpful to me because you weren't waiting until the end of the day or the end of the week to get feedback. You could literally walk out of a meeting after they've given you the reins for a little while, and you get to talk about it right away – what went right, what went wrong, what you could do better next time, different approaches you could take, etc. This way, you could incorporate the feedback into your very next meeting. This prevented issues and bad habits from festering – they were addressed and corrected right away, which was great for me.

The other benefit of the long drives was getting to know the established sales guys at a deeper level. I'm fortunate that I've been able to maintain many of the relationships that were formed on those trips to this day, with many remaining as friends and mentors even now.

"Great creators don't necessarily have the deepest expertise but rather seek out the broadest perspectives."
Adam Grant (American writer, *Originals: How Non-Conformists Move the World*, 2016)

LESSON 12:
Thinking Outside the Box

I was fortunate to be able to start my sales career in those early years with a few nice wins. These successes were largely a product of the quality of the company that I was working for, the skilled people they surrounded me, and hard work and being open to new ideas on my part. However they came, I was happy to have them, as they served to build a foundation of confidence under me.

As time went on, more challenging sales opportunities came my way. There's one sale that happened when I was two or three years into the role that I remember fondly to this day. This was an example of a conversation that led to a burgeoning (and unexpected) relationship that led to a sale and a long-term client relationship.

One day, I happened to be having a conversation with someone who I had met in a different industry – someone who seemingly had no need for the type of product we were pushing. However, you never know where a discussion is going to once two people start talking – and that was the case here.

This conversation was with an engineer that worked for a pharmaceutical company (which wasn't our target market). He was telling me about some interesting problems they were having in their clean rooms (for which we had no relevant products. Then, suddenly, a light bulb went off in my head. I blurted out, "I think we have a product that would fix that problem. It isn't marketed for that problem, but it does everything that you say it's going to need to do."

With that flash of inspiration, I went back to our team and worked closely with the engineering and product teams to customize a solution for a pharmaceutical clean room. Several months later, through our collective efforts, we turned the new product into an enormous sale.

This was good for me personally, as well as the company, for financial reasons, of course. Most importantly, though, it was a great "a-ha!" moment for me. It helped me realize that just because this product says it's for this particular use, it doesn't <u>only</u> have to be for that use. Simple, but true.

I've been fortunate to have had a few other, similar moments in my career. This was the first time that I really "got" the idea of trying to think "outside the box." Or perhaps better said, "Don't dismiss 'crazy' ideas when they come along. You never know – it might just work!"

It's a lesson that I've tried never to forget – especially when you're "stuck" on a problem and none of the tried-and-true solutions seem to be working. Speaking with a wide range of other people, sharing ideas, looking at a problem from all angles, and trying to take a different tack can bring new solutions – and sometimes, this pays off in huge dividends, as it did in this case.

I admit that it was a bit of an "ego boost" for me to come up with a solution that even the much more highly trained, educated, and astute engineers hadn't seen. (We'll take our small victories where they come!). Happily, I'm told that the company still uses the product for that application to this day, more than 20 years later. Here's to out-of-the-box thinking!

"To sell is to serve. Serve more, sell more."
Robin Sharma (Leadership Expert and Author, 2010s)

LESSON 13:
Diagnosing Problems and Helping People

I've learned that my job as a salesman isn't to be the loudest guy in the room. My job is to listen, to identify the problem, diagnose the situation, and provide a solution for the issue. When you can do all of that, that's when the "magic" happens. If other factors come together – like timing and the occasional stroke of good luck – then you have a very good chance to make a sale, and maybe even establish a long-term relationship with the customer.

Sometimes this happens in a very straightforward way, and sometimes not – it depends on the style and personalities of those involved. For example, in conversations, I tend to bounce around a little bit, but I get to the goal line when I need to. It's just I don't always take a straight line to get there. I just try to enjoy interacting with whomever I'm speaking with and go where the conversation takes us.

Others take a much more "linear" and logical approach – i.e., Point A leads to Point B leads to Point C. As long as we're both really listening and trying to understand the other's thoughts, we can often come together in the end with a great solution that neither of us would have arrived at on our own.

I was sharing with my kids recently that see myself as a "doctor" in certain ways (on a much less scientific level, of course). Sometimes, it's easy to tell what is ailing a patient; sometimes, it's harder to discern. You have to test. You have to probe. You have to ask questions to come up with a diagnosis. Once you have that, you need to provide a solution to the problem that's practical, realistic, and affordable. Happiness is when you can do all of that and really solve someone's problem.

I realize that this is a cliché, but I really do *love* helping people -- I always have, since I was a kid. And let's be honest -- it's good for me when I do that, too, because financially, that means that I've just won another customer, and that I'm going to be compensated for doing so. But what means the most to me is when I fix something for a customer and I see a smile on their face – or a burden lifted from their shoulders. Sometimes, when I'm lucky, I can even fix things on a long-term basis (like the example, above, of the clean room solution that still works 20 years later).

This is hard work and good fun, and it's all worth it in the end.

❖   ❖   ❖   ❖   ❖   ❖   ❖

"Humility is the solid foundation of all virtues."
Confucius (Chinese philosopher, 5th century B.C.)

LESSON 14:
Having Humility

One of the most difficult lessons that I've learned over the years is that there's not always a perfect solution. Those are often the trickiest situations to come to grips with – especially when it means that you're not the right person or company to fulfill the customer's needs. As the old Kenny Rogers song says, you've got to "know when to hold 'em and when to fold 'em." No one likes giving up short of the goal line – but sometimes, as painful to admit, that is the best answer for all involved.

There might be many reasons you can't solve the problem for the customer. One might be that science or technology hasn't found the answer yet. Another might be that another company has better solutions to the customer's needs than you do. Or sometimes one of the customer's stated desires is in conflict with one of their other desires and one need must be prioritized over another – which they may or may not be willing to do.

I've certainly been in customer-vendor relationships where there isn't always a perfect answer, despite the best efforts, intentions, and expertise of everyone in the situation. In these situations, taking the customer through your entire thought process and showing them exactly what alternatives are out there can serve to build long-term trust.

Sometimes, turning over all the rocks, so to speak, will spark a new answer, which is great! Other times, this will make it apparent that it is time for the customer to seek out vendors other than your company. Either way, you're giving the customer the best you have to offer out of imperfect alternatives, and it is up to them to decide what is in their best interests, as it should be.

Laying out these choices clearly is sometimes the best we can do, honestly. The hard part is having the humility to admit this to the customer and to yourself. It's not a "failing" and no one did anything "wrong" – it's just the reality that no one can be all things to all people. I never like walking away from a potential sale if there's even a glimmer of a chance of being able to help – but prudence tells us that it's sometimes the best course.

You have to be honest with yourself – and with the customer -- in these situations. It can be a real internal struggle, because you always want the sale (of course). Moreover, the natural competitor and problem-solver in you always believes that if you take just one more look at the situation, you'll have that "a-ha" moment where you find the perfect solution to their needs. In our imperfect world, though, sometimes this just isn't the case. That wasn't the easiest thing for me to learn – but it is true.

"Those who cannot remember the past are condemned to repeat it."
George Santayana (Novelist, *The Life of Reason*, 1905)

LESSON 15:
You Have to Learn Some Lessons Again

I know that it seems silly to say that "You should always know what day it is" – but, believe me, I learned this one the hard way. Like other lessons, I had to learn this several times before it finally "stuck" with me.

This goes back to 10-12 years into my career, when I was still with the industrial company that I had joined out of college. At that point, things had progressed to the point where I was traveling almost 45 weeks out of the year (no joke!) – so, I was on the road a lot more than I was at home. Being in a new place every day could get a little disorienting, in a "If it's Tuesday, this must be Pittsburgh" kind of way. Fortunately, I never forgot to come home (!) – but I have to admit to once (or twice) forgetting what day it was. Embarrassing, but true.

One Spring, I was working in Texas with our regional manager down there. We worked heavily with oil refineries and chemical plants at that point, and there was a big trade show for those guys at the end of the week on Friday. We organized our schedule so we could go do our own thing during the week and work the trade show together on Friday.

That plan worked fine – until we got to the trade show and found out that some of our samples weren't there. We were trying to get a hold of the local Houston office or the headquarters out on the east coast and couldn't reach anyone.

As this is all going on, one of the guys running the show walks by, and he says, "Hey, I want to thank you guys so much. It's not easy to get people to show up on Good Friday." We realized at that point that our company was closed on Good Friday, which is why no one was available.

That was funny enough – but then we fast forward to the next year, and we did the same thing, again! I had forgotten to check the calendar again. Sometimes, lessons need to be learned multiple times, I guess.

The happy news is that we ended up doing very well at those shows. Since not a lot of vendors were there due to the holiday scheduling, we had plenty of time to chat with everyone who was there. A relaxed atmosphere (i.e., no time pressures) ... led to better conversations ... led to establishing closer initial relationships ... led to more potential sales. Resilience – and not knowing how to read a calendar! – worked in our favor in that case.

❖   ❖   ❖   ❖   ❖   ❖   ❖

"Learning is not attained by chance, it must be sought for with ardor and diligence."
Abigail Adams (Revolutionary War figure, wife and correspondent of John Adams – 2nd U.S. President)

LESSON 16:
Learn Everything You Can About Your Profession

In the early days of my sales career, I had the benefit of great sales mentors, and I drew important "on the job" lessons from them. Thinking about it now, I probably relied on this too exclusively, though. I would have benefitted from a little more "self-study" in the sense that, there are a lot of great sales books and videos out there that I didn't take advantage of early on – which was a missed (or at least, delayed) opportunity.

It's true that I was soaking in as much practical knowledge as I could from seeing things happen live that I then tried to put into practice in my next conversation. And it's also true that materials weren't quite as available as they are today, where every sales approach that has ever been created can be studied on YouTube and other sites, often for free. Even so, I could have done a much better job of seeking and absorbing the materials that were available much earlier in my career.

Gurus, teachers, and techniques -- Eventually, over the course of the years, I've been exposed to more of the "sales gurus", though, and I've probably come to use every one of the main sales methods that are out there – e.g., SPIN selling, Challenge Sales, the Sandler Method, etc. Necessarily, I've blended many of these techniques into a unique approach that works best for me. My general idea is to be as knowledgeable as possible about all the best techniques and use the one that will work best in the particular situation that I'm in.

One caveat: Sometimes in my career, I've known salespeople who use one technique only, regardless of whether it might be the most effective approach for the situation. I think it's best to be "agnostic," though – i.e., use what works best in the situation, which rarely means taking the same approach over and over and over again, regardless of circumstances. Most often, taking a varied approach – which we'll talk about in more detail in the following lessons, below – will be the ticket to success.

❖   ❖   ❖   ❖   ❖   ❖   ❖

"When we allow ourselves to adapt to different situations, life is easier."
Catherine Pulsifer (Canadian writer, *Wings of Wisdom*)

LESSON 17:
Fitting the Approach to the Situation

As I progressed in my sales career and got into my late 20s and early 30s, I started going to some sales seminars. (This was pre-COVID, when they still held seminars in-person rather than exclusively on Zoom). I was lucky enough that the industrial company I was working for would send me to these seminars to see what I thought was good and wasn't good, and I ran into a few that resonated with me.

In terms of written materials, there's a wonderful book out there called *The Challenger Sale* (by Matthew Dixon, Brent Adamson, et al). I found that approach to be among the most interesting, because it's actually taking almost every one of those other sales methodologies and using it in different situations, which is what I feel fits my sales and communication style the best.

I think the really good -- and certainly the great -- sales people use several different sales methods because you're not talking to the same person in all conversations. From customer to customer, you're dealing with different people with different agendas and different needs. You need to be able to identify who you're dealing with, what they're looking for, how they take in information, and what's likely to propel them to act (or to walk away).

Are you talking to an analytical person? Are you talking to somebody that's looking for an advisor or consultant? Are you talking to somebody that just has these six specific problems and wants them fixed. You need to be aware of who it is that you're speaking to, and you need to cater to that person, if you want to be successful in the sales process with them.

If you try to take the same sales approach with the CFO as with the CEO as with the HR Director, you'll likely struggle to connect with at least one (if not all) of them. Success requires you to know, understand, and be skilled in multiple approaches. The good news is that, by applying yourself diligently over a relatively short period of time, the information is available for you to master and to use to your sales benefit.

In doing so, you'll be furthering your relationships with all involved – with each believing that you "get them" because you "speak their language," give them what they need to know, and point them toward a solution they can understand and believe in. You might not close every sale this way – but you certainly give yourself your best shot at doing so, in my opinion.

❖   ❖   ❖   ❖   ❖   ❖   ❖

"Luck is what happens when preparation meets opportunity."
Seneca (Roman philosopher, 1st Century AD)

LESSON 18:
Keeping Your Career Exciting

While my career didn't always remain as exciting as it was the first couple years (few things do), I was lucky enough to be recognized by the company and receive small promotions and role changes every few years – which helped to keep things fresh. The fact that I was never in the same role for an extended period helped keep things new and not boring.

After starting my career in the Kansas City territory, I was able to move back to Chicago with the same company. Being back on my "home turf" in Chicagoland was a blast, and I was covering different states with new customers for several years. I was then promoted to a more managerial position as a Market Segment Manager and later became a Product Manager. In this way, I was happily able to stay with the same great company while still progressing in my career.

After about a dozen years with the industrial company, I left to move into the insurance industry (more about that, below). All told, I feel very fortunate that I was only with two companies my entire professional career (25 years) before founding my own firm recently. This type of stability isn't so common these days, and I'm thankful for it, especially being able to experience growth all the while – which certainly provided a breath of fresh air and sense of progress at key moments.

❖   ❖   ❖   ❖   ❖   ❖   ❖

"The difference between a successful person and others is not a lack of strength, not a lack of knowledge, but rather a lack in will."
Vince Lombardi (Hall of Fame Coach,
Green Bay Packers, 1960s)

LESSON 19:
The Value of Persistence

Whether it's a television ad or an Instagram or Facebook or other social media post, every day we see messages about "never giving up." A real-life example of this comes to mind from a long time ago, when I was in the industrial manufacturing world.

As I've mentioned, when I was in my first sales role, I relocated to Kansas City. After I completed the company's training program, it was time to go out and: 1 - service the existing customers, and 2 - find new customers to grow the business.

As we'll discuss later in the "Hunter and Farmer" lesson, finding new customers was always a fun challenge for me. One prospective customer in Kansas always sticks out in my mind that exemplifies "the thrill of the hunt" – and, most importantly, the need to be persistent and resilient. Here's that story.

This was right at the beginning of the 2000s, when the internet was just starting to take-hold. So, we were still going into phone books to find sales prospects. Grabbing the thick Yellow Pages book, I would look up local distributors to set up appointments to visit in the area that I was focusing on that week. I would always call in advance to try to get a meeting – and, even if I couldn't get a meeting, I would stop by just to try to learn a little bit more about their business.

With that set up, there was one prospect that I could never get to call me back. I visited their offices a couple of times, and no one was unavailable to see me. Keep in mind, seeing them required a road trip – they were located a few hours away from my home base in Kansas City. So, without an overnight stay, it wasn't the most convenient place to just stop by and chat.

It started driving me crazy that I couldn't get a meeting in this company because the more I learned about them, the more I knew the sale would be a slam dunk. They were existing customers of sorts, in that they were buying some of our products through another distributor. I knew that it would benefit them to buy directly from us, and I felt we could be doing even more business with them. The worst part was, I knew that they had a lot of my competitors' products in their facility – which is what drove me nuts.

Finally, I got the name of the owner of the company, so I at least could try to schedule a meeting with him. I was probably six or seven months into the job when I finally got a meeting with him. I showed up for the meeting, and the secretary let me know that he wasn't available.

I said, "Oh, is he running late?"

"No," she replied pleasantly, "he's not going to be here today."

"Okay, great," I thought. "Well, I was only in town for that day, so I'll try again another time."

Fast forward a few months. I set up the appointment again and showed up on the appointed day. The secretary says, "Oh, I'm sorry. He's not available today."

I explained (again), "We had a meeting scheduled on this day at this time."

"I'm sorry. He's not going to be here today." Okay.

I leave again, and this happens two more times. It's to the point where my blood is boiling, and I don't understand why this is happening or what the disconnect is here. So, I set up the fifth meeting. I confirm it three times, making sure that I'm going to be there at the right time on the right date. He should have no excuse for missing the meeting this time.

When I arrived for the fifth time, the owner was at the secretary's desk. I thought in my head, "This is going to be interesting for him to try not to take the meeting."

Much to my surprise, the owner just had a big smile on his face and said, "George, I'm glad you're here."

I said, "Well, I'm glad _you're_ here," and we had a laugh together.

He said, "I didn't want to drive you nuts, but I get calls from sales guys all the time, always looking for meetings. Until somebody shows up five times, I will not talk to them." That was just his standing rule where he would not see anybody before their fifth visit.

It was his way of seeing whether the salesperson was serious and worth his time. OK, then – lesson learned!

The funnier part was when he said, "Oh, by the way -- your father used to call on me 30 years ago." It turns out he was a customer of my dad's when my Dad was in a different company. So, I had faith that you would come back as long as was needed."

Fast forward a few years, and they became a very good customer of ours.

It taught me a lot about perseverance and working through things. I don't want to say it was about "not taking no for an answer," because it was never a "No." It was just, "Not now" or "Not yet." The lesson is really about not getting overly frustrated when obstacles or delays arise and the importance of sticking with your plan until it comes to fruition.

It was a good lesson for me to learn early on because I'm not a pushy person, but I'm also not a person that's going to give up on things. It taught me a lot about what can happen when you don't get flustered and keep showing up. Being persistent can lead to a lot of good outcomes.

It's also a reminder that there are often things going on in a situation which aren't visible to you – in the same way that we don't see an entire ice cube (or an iceberg, for that matter) if we don't look below the waterline. I thought that the owner was just canceling the appointments randomly, but he had a whole plan that I wasn't aware of. I'm glad that I had the patience to stick it out in this case. It often makes all the difference in the world.

❖   ❖   ❖   ❖   ❖   ❖   ❖

*"If you can make them laugh,
you can make them listen."*
John C. Maxwell (Leadership expert and author,
Everyone Communicates, Few Connect, 2010)

LESSON 20:
Presenting to Large and Small Groups

I've learned that sometimes others view your strengths differently than you do. For example, I'm always surprised that I get complimented a lot on group presentations. Based on feedback, this is probably one of my stronger suits. Even though I don't feel it is a strength, it seems to be where I get a lot of praise. Go figure!

When I first started in sales, my mentors at the industrial company certainly stressed the importance of "being comfortable on my feet" in front of groups – which is a bedrock requirement for most successful salespeople. Any skills that I've acquired in this area – beyond natural ability – go back to the I've got what feel like 8 million examples of great presentations that I've seen given – by my dad and other of my early sales mentors.

We'll get to my dad and other mentors in a moment. I wanted to start, though, by going back further in time to one other person that I have to give a lot of credit to -- my high school Speech teacher, Mr. Arellano. He had the unenviable task of try to teach 14, 15, 16-year-old kids how to communicate effectively. Fortunately for us, he had a passion for this, and he was great at it!

Mr. Arellano taught us not only how to get comfortable in front of the room, but how to really drive the speech -- how to make eye contact with people, how to control the room, even when things are getting out of control. So, at an early age, I had a lot of examples of how to give presentations, which has been a great benefit to me throughout the years. While I've lost touch with him over the years, Mr. Arellano, if you happen to be reading this, please know how much of a difference your efforts have made in my life.

The funny thing is, I still get nervous giving presentations, but I think I've done enough of them to where it just becomes second nature. And even though I might be a nervous wreck on the inside, I'm told that I manage to look calm and composed on the outside. There's a lot to be said for the "fake it until you make it" philosophy, at least regarding public speaking!

Getting back to my dad, I quickly saw from our road trips that presenting to groups was one of his greatest strengths. Dad had a natural skill for commanding a room, and his presentations were electric, but the truth is that the products he was talking about were not very exciting. In fact, they were very boring products -- so he had to work extra hard to keep people's attention, which is where this "lesson" comes in.

After taking a few trips with him, I noticed a few "tricks of the trade" that he relied on – and I've tried to adapt some of these in my own presentations.

Dad always carried a briefcase with him, which was separate from the sample pack of (again, boring) products he was selling. The briefcase was different – it was just a bunch of nonsensical items that he knew that he would need at some point to get people re-energized and reinvigorated. There was a flamethrowing magic wand in there, along with a fake "hand grenade," as well as any number of other fun toys, gadgets, and gizmos. When he saw people's eyes glazing over (which was inevitable, despite his best efforts), he could pull something out to make them smile or laugh – which just about always worked.

One time that I remember was when I was probably 11 or 12 years old and we were in a meeting in Ohio. It wasn't one of his bigger presentations, but there were 30 or 40 people in the room. I must admit my eyes were glazing over as a 12-year-old, and he started losing some of the customers. Suddenly, I see him going for the briefcase and I knew something good was going to happen.

Out of nowhere, a rubber chicken went flying across the table. Then, with a starter pistol in his hand, he popped off three shots of the pistol. Just about everybody in the room had a heart attack -- and there was a huge laugh afterwards. He definitely had their attention again!

Now, this was back in the 1980s, when it was a little easier to get away with some unorthodox stuff. I don't think you could do that in 2025 anymore, but with the group he was with, it was well timed and certainly got their attention back into the meeting. Besides livening things up, I think it was also his way of acknowledging, "Hey, I know this isn't the most thrilling topic. I appreciate your attention and want to brighten your day for a minute." And I'm sure it gave a few people a story to tell around the family dinner table that night.

It was all in good fun, of course – but had an important purpose, too. If people remember you enough to tell stories about you at the dinner table, that's never a bad thing for a salesperson.

❖   ❖   ❖   ❖   ❖   ❖   ❖

"Laughter is the shortest distance between two people."
Victor Borge (Comedian and pianist, 1950s)

LESSON 21:
Responding with Grace and Humor

Staying with the need for "being good on your feet" as a salesperson, I wanted to share one other example I remember from my time on the road with my dad that had a big impact on me. It combined several lessons about commanding a room, being comfortable in your own skin, and having the grace and humility to poke fun at yourself.

This happened to be one of the bigger presentations I saw him give, where there were probably a few hundred people in the audience. He was working for a large manufacturer and had just switched over from a competitor with a very similar name. In the presentation, Dad accidentally said the name of his former company just out of habit before catching himself. No big deal, of course – "no harm, no foul," as they say, and the audience graciously understood.

This particular day, there happened to be a pitcher of water in front him, so that he could "wet his whistle" if he got dry during the presentation (this was in the days before there were always water bottles at every meeting or presentation). After the third or fourth time he said the old company's name, he looked at the crowd and said, "If I say (the other name) one more time, I'm going to pour this pitcher of water on my head."

Sure enough, five minutes later, he said the wrong name again. Without missing a beat, he picked up the pitcher and poured it right over his head -- and then continued with his presentation for another hour as if nothing unusual had happened. The audience roared in reaction – and again, more stories of the "you'll never believe what I saw today" variety were shared over dinner tables that evening.

Seeing those things in my youth was a great memory and certainly had a big impact on me. It showed me that you have to be comfortable in front of any crowd – including being secure in the knowledge that you're going to "mess up" from time to time. The key thing is, how are you going to recover from those mistakes when you're in these presentations? Will it be by getting flustered and losing your place (and losing the crowd)? Or will it be with some soft, self-deprecating humor, like Dad did with his "pouring water over his head" diversion? One way is much more memorable and impactful than the other, of course.

I think we've all seen somebody who has trouble with the presentation, and they start to fumble and fall apart -- which is painful for all concerned and as a presenter is the last thing you want to happen. Recovering smoothly from mishaps is a very important skill that comes from practice and experience – i.e., you need to be ready with a backup plan.

For example, if the PowerPoint fails, you need to be able to do that presentation without that PowerPoint. As long as you're prepared, there's nothing to be embarrassed by. Your audience will almost always "forgive" glitches if you show them the respect of having prepared properly and adjusting on the fly.

Always remember that a little self-deprecating humor goes a long way. I've learned that humility will have people laughing with you rather than laughing at you.

❖   ❖   ❖   ❖   ❖   ❖   ❖

"Pay less attention to what men say. Just watch what they do."
Dale Carnegie (Author and motivator, circa 1936)

LESSON 22:
Going the Extra Mile (Literally)

Most of the "lessons" that we've discussed so far have been "serious" in nature. Since it's my nature to try to keep the mood "light" whenever possible, I wanted to mix in a story at this point that is just flat-out "fun" – or, at least, it was fun for me.

When I was working for the industrial company, I had a unique experience that I'll never forget. It involved me doing something (obtaining a CDL, commercial driver's license) that I never would have imagined.

The company had hundreds of thousands of products, which made it difficult to show off all our products at trade shows. One of the marketing people had the great idea to have a trailer specially built for us where we could display our featured products – like a showroom on wheels for the sales team. (This was a great example of "out of the box" thinking that we were talking about earlier). It was Featherlite custom made 46-foot trailer that was over 30,000 pounds. Because of the weight, you had to have a CDL to operate it. A few years later, they had a second one built because we had so much success with the first one.

When we were looking at the trade show calendar for the year, we realized that at one point in the year, we needed it to get the trailer from Atlanta to Wisconsin Dells in a very short period. Seeing the opportunity for a neat experience, I volunteered to take the wheel. Since you had to get a CDL license to drive it, I went out about a month prior and got my CDL license. The other important aspect of the story is that with a truck that size, there are Federal DOT rules that come with it – such as, you can only be behind the wheel for something like 10 out of 12 hours in a day (or whatever the standard was at that time).

I had to get it from Atlanta to the Wisconsin Dells, and we had probably 20 hours to do it. This seems like plenty of time, but it's a 13- or 14-hour drive before you factor in the DOT time-driven restrictions. However, I hit the road, and it was going great – until, as I'm going through the Smoky Mountains, a nice blizzard decided to roll in. I kept moving -- but instead of driving 50 or 60 miles an hour, I'm going more like eight to ten miles an hour, which made the trip even longer and tightened the timeline. But we got it done.

I still remember pulling into the parking lot in Wisconsin Dells – where, if you haven't been, they have a bunch of indoor water parks, casinos, and nice family vacation places. The way that I felt pulling in there – after what seemed like an "epic" journey to me -- I was waiting for a parade to meet me and all these people to be applauding. Of course, I pulled in and nobody other than me cared. (Nor should they have – they were on vacation and didn't know what the unusual trailer in the parking lot was all about, of course). I knew that our team cared – they were waiting for me and were super excited that I was there so that they could do what they needed to do at the tradeshow.

For me, though, it was exciting, and I was proud to get it done. I like a challenge, and I love being able to prove that hard things can be done -- instead of just saying, "No." As a salesperson (and a competitive person), you always want to get to "Yes." Happily, this time, that's exactly what happened.

❖   ❖   ❖   ❖   ❖   ❖   ❖

"Mentoring someone is not creating them in your own image but giving them the opportunity to create themselves."
Steven Spielberg (Academy Award-Winning filmmaker)

LESSON 23:
Managing Accounts and Managing Others

After several years in stand-alone sales roles, I was put in charge of National Accounts for the first time. This job had a different feel for me for a few reasons. The first was because I had been dealing with all local or regional customers, it was a learning experience for me to see customers from a national perspective. At the same time, this role involved managing a team, which was new for me at the time, as well.

I had been a "lone wolf" for my entire career up jumping into the managerial role. I had been on sales teams as well as sports teams growing up, and I had experienced some great managers and some so-so managers. Now I was a manager myself – which was more of a challenge for me than I had anticipated.

As an "individual contributor," I had relied solely on myself until then. I was just good at getting things done and making sure that my customers' needs were taken care of. Now, as a manager, I had to get things done through other people, while also teaching them the best ways to support their customers and grow their books of business. I soon realized that I had a lot to learn to be even mildly proficient as a manager.

After a while, I started to figure out this managing a team thing a little more. I began to realize that if we were truly a team, I had to start acting like it and I had to trust the team members to do what they did best. This meant that I had to release the reins a little bit and let them do their job without my constant oversight, so that they could learn by doing – even if how they were doing it wasn't exactly how I would have done it. It took a good couple months to figure that out – mostly by trial and error -- which felt like a very long time at the time.

I was frustrated because I felt that I should have been able to learn how to be a manager much quicker than I did. Happily, though, eventually I realized that I had to model trust and believe in the team, and act accordingly. I had to remember that my job was to do the "guiding" and they were really the front-line "doers." When that finally "clicked" for me, I became much better at the management side of things.

Once I saw this was starting to work, I said to myself, "Okay. These guys are as good, if not better than me. If I can help grow their skills while growing their book of business, we should be fine." That was my plan, at least – and happily, it ended up working.

One way I tried to do this was to demonstrate a few different sales techniques when I had them "ride along" with me on a customer visit – then I set them free to lead the customer meeting the next time out. This way, they could practice what I had taught them, and we could assess how it went afterward. This was exactly what the senior salespeople had done with me when I was just starting out.

Seeing that work well a few times and come to fruition on some deals was eye-opening. While being a manager 100-percent of the time is not my favorite thing to do – I like being the one out there on the front line -- it's certainly something I was able to do, and it became much more enjoyable the more I did it well.

❖ ❖ ❖ ❖ ❖ ❖ ❖

"True humility is staying teachable, regardless of how much you already know."
Anonymous

LESSON 24:
Learning from Your Mentee

They say that the best mentor – mentee relationship is one where both parties learn from each other. One story that illustrates this point comes from the early days of my management career. It involves a young sales team member from the Southeast who I had always really enjoyed working with him. To this day, I think he's a better salesperson than I am. I don't know if he knows that, but it's true.

While he was on my team, I felt like he looked up to me as a "learned elder," which is always a nice feeling. The funny thing about it is, at the same time, I was kind of looking up to him because – I have to admit -- I was a little jealous of some of his skills. He had a very natural way of directing a meeting exactly the way that it should be run without ever upsetting the customers. He had a great personality and a great ability to listen and give very well-thought-out responses to whatever he was asked.

I always felt proud working with him just because he was so wonderful at what he did. I would always try to give him little tips and tricks of the trade – but the truth is, I was never really sure how much I was helping him, as he was already very polished at a young age.

As a very polite young man (his parents clearly raised him right), he was always very thankful to me for helping him – while I'm laughing in my head because I'm learning as much, if not more, from him than he might be learning from me. Seeing him continue to thrive in his career was a very prideful moment for me. That sticks out for me, all these years later.

❖   ❖   ❖   ❖   ❖   ❖   ❖

"To be yourself in a world that is constantly trying to make you something else is the greatest accomplishment."
Ralph Waldo Emerson (American essayist, 1841)

LESSON 25:
Balancing Career and Family Isn't Easy

One of my least favorite memories comes from my last few years with the industrial company. At that time, I was traveling about 42 to 45 weeks a year. This is true "road warrior" status – but, believe me, it's nothing to be proud of and isn't a good way to live, for most people. And it wasn't a good way for me to live anymore, either.

For Context -- In the middle of my run with the industrial company, I had met a lovely young lady, fallen madly in love, and got married. A few years later, we had our first child (and later, a second child) – all of which are the most important things in my life by far. (Much more about them, later)

Now, back to our story.

Getting Off the Travel Hamster Wheel -- It wasn't that the company was pushing me to stay on the road. I had very good bosses and they were trying to pull the reins back on me, to get me off the road and keep me at home more. The struggle, though, was that to do the best job I could and be good at it, I felt that I needed to be face-to-face with the customers and prospects -- in my way of thinking, at least. I was working directly with engineers inside of chemical plants and oil refineries, and I really felt that I needed to be with them in person to truly help them solve their problems. So, I was pushing myself.

I was traveling virtually every week in those days. I would leave on Monday mornings – or sometimes even Sunday evenings -- and get back home on Thursday nights or Friday mornings. My daughter was still very young, but she started to realize how often I'd be gone. I remember one time when I was packing my bag on a Sunday night in my bedroom, getting ready to leave, and she just started crying. That absolutely stuck with me, and I realized that maybe I needed to be open to some changes.

For me personally, it was a lot easier traveling when I was single. It was still relatively easy when I was married without kids. Once I had a family, it became more difficult for me. Sure, I was the main bread winner and was responsible for putting food on the table. However, it wasn't worth very much to my wonderful wife and children if this meant that they never saw their husband and father.

Fortunate Timing - As luck would have it, at about that same time, a friend of mine had just started their own insurance agency, and they were recruiting me to come along because they believed that I would be good fit. My friend -- who is also a great salesperson-- pitched me on the idea that sales is a skill that is transferable between industries, which I believe, too. He had been with me enough in a variety of situations and had seen how I interacted with individuals and groups to come to conclusion that I'd be very successful in his industry – which was very kind and an ego boost.

Making the Leap -- I was very fortunate that, being connected to as many people as I was, there were jobs being offered all the time. It was an eye-opening moment for me when I realized, "Alright, there are other opportunities here where I don't have to be on the road all the time."

In my professional life, that was the scariest decision that I ever had to make up to that point. I went with my gut, though, and ended up accepting the position with my friend and his insurance agency, where I'm happy to report that I had a very successful and rewarding run for almost a decade.

I'm very grateful that things worked out the way that they did, particularly regarding travel. I still traveled a little bit with the insurance agency (and still today, with my own firm), but usually in much more planned way. I would travel maybe twice a quarter -- usually for a day or two or maybe three days max.

It's nice sleeping in your own bed and, most importantly, it's been a great benefit to see my family on a regular basis. I feel like I've seen my kids grow up in a much more meaningful and present way than would have been possible being on the road 40+ weeks a year.

Everyone must make their own decisions and chart their own paths, of course. For me and my family, though, there's no doubt in my mind that this was the right course for me.

> ***"It's what you learn after you know it all that counts."***
> John Wooden (UCLA basketball coach,
> *They Call Me Coach*, 1972)

LESSON 26:
Learning a New Industry

Sales is a transferrable skill, in that the basics are the same everywhere – i.e., identifying customer needs, proposing solutions, negotiating prices, closing the deal, etc. However, one of the key aspects of changing industries is, of course, learning the new industry and understanding what makes that industry different from other fields.

Working for an industrial company for all those years, I had to be very aware of how our product were designed to be used in terms of safety, compliance to regulations, exposure to liability, and all that "fun" (i.e., boring but important) stuff. It may be surprising to hear me say this, but having had exposure to that world made it relatively easy for me to transition into commercial insurance, because insurance (and more specifically, risk management and compliance) often came into conversations with my industrial clients

Beyond learning about the industry itself, there is the question about learning about your target audience – i.e., your current and prospective customers. During my time with the industrial company, I was specifically targeting engineers and plant managers. When I moved into the insurance world, I understood right away that I had to shift my focus considerably, as engineers and plant managers are obviously not the people that are making insurance decisions in most cases. Depending on the size of the company and whether we're talking about commercial insurance or health benefits, my key customer contacts are now Human Resources VPs, Benefits Directors, Chief Financial Officers, and CEOs.

So, those are some of the differences that I had to adjust to when changing industries. Where, then, did the "transferability of skills" come into play? Here, the key similarity turned out to be the fact that in sales, regardless of industry, the main job is to build good, strong relationships (thus, the title of this book).

In the industrial world, I was always comfortable dealing with ownership and the Operations executives of our customers. Now, I had to add HR and Finance leaders to my repertoire -- to understand their needs and perspectives and build rapport with them. Fortunately, I was able to draw on my general relationship building skills and natural curiosity – and I soon found myself very comfortable in my new world of insurance.

Before we bring the story up to the present day -- We'll talk a lot more about my decade-plus in the insurance industry in the next section. Before we get there, though, I wanted to share a few pictures that cover my early career years as well as customer and event pictures from my time in the insurance industry. I've also included a few family snapshots, as family is everything, and they've certainly played a huge role in my career.

MID-CAREER & FAMILY PHOTOS

From whom it all began – a special dinner with my dad.

A quasi-official headshot from my early days at the industrial company

My wife, Laura, and I with our daughter during her first visit with Mickey and Minnie

Having fun at a golf/fundraising event with friends

Laura and I enjoying a "date night" on the town

Closing a deal with good customers in their offices

Dinner with one of my closest friends from high school (and a customer!)

Having fun in tiny chairs at a sales call at a private school for young kids

Cubs game with one of my old bosses and another salesman, both mentors of mine

Coaching my son's youth basketball team

SECTION 3:
LOOKING BACK AND FORWARD

Now that we've talked about my childhood and the early career experiences that were so foundational for me, I'd like to use this final section of the book to bring the story full-circle by bring you up to speed on the past dozen years while also sharing key lessons that have been reinforced in me throughout my career.

As we'll see, the names and places may change over the course of time, but everything inevitably harkens back to the principles that were ingrained in me early on. We'll wrap things up with lessons that I've learned most recently in my newest role as CEO/Founder of my own agency.

❖   ❖   ❖   ❖   ❖   ❖   ❖

"Faith is taking the first step even when you don't see the whole staircase."
Martin Luther King Jr. (Civil rights leader,
Speech in Montgomery, 1962)

LESSON 27:
Stepping Outside Your Comfort Zone

Throughout my life and career, I've seen the benefit of trying new things and taking leaps of faith (within reason), particularly when starting out in a new role or unfamiliar situation. There is always a certain fear when venturing into the unknown. Sometimes, however, you sense right away that the new circumstance was tailor-made for you and you're immediately confident of your success. In either case, I've found that it's best to analyze the situation and then stand tall and move forward with confidence into the unknown.

As one example, I was honored when a business contact (himself, a new business owner/founder) invited me to participate in his new golf-based podcast where he interviews CEOs and business executives as they play a round of golf. The premise is "Nine holes. Nine questions about your industry," which is a neat set-up. Given my golfing background, I couldn't pass it up.

I was a little hesitant because I've never done something exactly like that before on camera. At the same time, chatting about business on the golf course is something that I've done my whole adult life -- so it wasn't too great a stretch for me. It seemed pretty low-risk -- i.e., if it didn't turn out well, he didn't have to post it on social media. Also, our interests were aligned, in that we both wanted the content to be as interesting as possible, for both our brands. So, I was happy to take this small "leap" and decided I would give it my best shot.

While we hadn't known each other in-depth prior to the podcast, it turns out that the host is very easy to talk with and we really hit it off on the course (pardon the pun). It was a lot of fun, and I'm happy with the way it turned out.

It was a pretty cool experience to see how a few hours of filming came together in a cohesive program. No one likes how they look or sound on the screen, of course – but, my family approved, so I guess it wasn't too bad or embarrassing. The moral of the story is that taking calculated risks – i.e., small leaps of faith – is often a good strategy. Small leaps can often turn into important building blocks for future success, further building your confidence to take larger leaps with potentially bigger rewards.

The adage "Nothing ventured, nothing gained" really is true!

❖ ❖ ❖ ❖ ❖ ❖ ❖

"Take a giant leap into that which sets your soul on fire and never retire from that leap."
— Hiral Nagda (Indian author and entrepreneur, 2024)

LESSON 28:
Having the Courage to Go Out on Your Own

After almost a decade in the insurance business, I started to get a feeling that it might be time for another big change in my career. It had been a great run with a great company, and I'll always be grateful for having the opportunity to contribute to their significant growth and development during this period.

At the same time, I recalled the words in the Bible about there being "to everything a season – a time to reap, and a time to sew" (Ecclesiastes 3:1), and it just felt like the right time to change this up a bit. After heartfelt discussions with my family, everyone was onboard, and I decided to make the leap and found my own firm.

It was scary to start planning to go out on my own after being part of teams and organizations my entire career. At the same time, there was an underlying confidence that I knew it was the right time to do it. I had a vision for what I wanted to be doing. And I was in a place where I could take advantage of my situation to go ahead and do something on my own. I'm extremely excited about it. Luckily, we're off to a good start, which calms the nerves considerably.

Below are some of the lessons that I've learned so far from venturing out on my own – plus some "classic" lessons that I've re-learned and experienced again from the early days of my career.

❖   ❖   ❖   ❖   ❖   ❖   ❖

"You miss 100 percent of the shots you don't take."
Wayne Gretzky (NHL Hall of Famer, 1983)

LESSON 29:
What I've Learned from Starting My Own Firm

As you may imagine, starting my own firm has caused (or required) me to draw on all my skills and lessons learned from the past. It has been a daunting and also exhilarating task – and I wouldn't trade it for the world!

The first few weeks and months were absolute madness getting everything set up, because not only were we bringing on customers, but we were getting the back-end systems in place at the same time. Two key insights that I've gained from this process so far are:

1 – *You'll never be completely ready ... but take the leap anyway (or else, you never will).* While I've always tried to be prudent in my career and life plans, by nature I'm an action-oriented person who is willing to take risks if there is the likelihood of bettering my situation for my family and myself. In the period leading up to going out on my own, I tried to map out what I needed to have in place for a successful launch – including both "systems" (e.g., operating software, website, legal structure, etc.); and "personal communications" (e.g., gaining my family's buy-in and support, as well as wrapping things up amicably with my prior employer who I hold in high regard); and promotional plans (e.g., notifying past contacts and prospective clients).

I'll admit that it has been a great challenge to pull together – as they say, "Be careful what you wish for. You may get it!" I have tried to remember that we were never going to be completely "ready" and there was never going to be the "perfect" time to launch. So, I did as much as I could do in preparation ... and then made the leap. And I'm happy to say that we've never looked back!

2 – Put systems in place as a foundation of support (and trust the experts to run them)

While much of sales is about relationships, you still need to be organized, of course, so that you keep all your appointments and commitments in a professional manner. In addition, a system is needed to "keep the train on the rails" and ensure that your operations support customers' needs in exactly the way you've promised.

As with many with "natural sales personalities," I'm good enough at operations to get by, but it's not my natural strength. Therefore, I've been very fortunate to find talented operations and subject matter experts to carry out the day to day "blocking and tackling" that is so crucial for a business to survive and thrive.

After learning lessons about the need to delegate earlier in my career, I have no problem giving responsibility to those whose operational talents are much more developed than my own. Happily, we've got terrific people in place and we're ready to rock.

We're growing at a very steady pace in our first year of operations, and we've already had several large customers sign on, exceeding my initial estimates. We keep plowing ahead and things are moving in a very good direction. Full speed ahead!

❖   ❖   ❖   ❖   ❖   ❖   ❖

"Culture eats strategy for breakfast."
Attributed to Peter Drucker (management guru, author)

LESSON 30:
Building the Right Culture for Your Team

Ever since the COVID pandemic occurred – and probably pre-dating that by a few years – there's been an ongoing discussion in the workplace and in our culture about "working from home" (aka, "remote work," "hybrid schedules," and other similar terms). While there are many thoughtful points of view on this issue, for our team, we have come down squarely on the side of remote work, which we've all been doing since we launched our new venture. This came about for a few different reasons:

- It is everybody's preference right now – so, it is good for morale, which is particularly important for a new company, helping us launch with high energy and spirit

- Given that I'm handling sales, I'm generally in clients' offices anyway – so, it would be silly to force our team members to come to "headquarters" every day (incurring commuting time, cost, and aggravation) when I'm not often in the office anyway. ("Do as I say, not as I do" is rarely a good management strategy, I've found).

- While I absolutely believe that moments of inspiration and great new ideas often stem from "chatting around the watercooler" (as was the term in the old days), I'm "modern" enough to realize that this can just as easily happen on a Zoom call or a WhatsApp thread these days as it can in-person. The important part is the communication itself, not necessarily where it takes place.

- As long as we can all serve customers in the ways they want to be supported, that's all that's important – not where we do it from. I'm lucky enough to have a nice office at my house, where I'm happy to retreat to after a day of customer visits – and where I can comfortably handle Zoom calls and presentations, as business dictates. The same is true for each of our team members.

Eventually, as we continue to grow, I'm sure that it will make sense for us to hang our shingle on an office building – probably with a mix of in-office and at-home days each week. For right now, a fully remote work arrangement fits our culture, operations, and communications styles very well.

❖   ❖   ❖   ❖   ❖   ❖   ❖

"Tell me and I forget, teach me and I may remember, involve me and I learn."
Benjamin Franklin (American statesman, *Poor Richard's Almanack*, 1750s)

LESSON 31:
Brings Others Along for Their Benefit

They say that "exposure" is sometimes the best form of mentoring, and I agree. Like my experiences mentioned earlier of "going on the road" with my dad, it's neat being on the opposite side of that equation these days, where I'm in a position to involve and expose my kids to business situations in different ways. Here's just one example.

Recently, one of my customers invited my daughter to come along when I visited their location. The customer is a large animal protection organization, and my 14-year-old daughter is a big lover of animals. Their shelter is actually where we adopted our family dog. When my daughter heard where I was going, she asked if she could come with me, so I gave the customer a call just to be sure that it would be ok.

She was thrilled when they said, "We'd love to have her come down and help out while you're here." Upon our arrival, they quickly put her to work, passing out leaflets, shelter information, and the like. When I was done with my meeting, we got to spend a little time with the dogs and almost ended up leaving with another one!

It was one of the first times I was able to have one of my children involved in what I do for a living, which was great. It brought a smile to her face, which brought a bigger smile to my face. I can't wait to do more of this.

Not wanting to be left out of the fun, my son has started asking where he can go with me and what he can do. He's already a good golfer at a young age, so he wants to play golf with a customer – another example of the "circle of life" repeating itself, you could say, given my own golfing background.

Having my kids involved brings me back to those days when I was able to tag along with my dad and absorb the experience of how he did what he did for a living – which I'm sure had a great deal to do with what my brother and I ended up doing for living.

❖   ❖   ❖   ❖   ❖   ❖   ❖

> *You can't control the wind, but you can control your sails.*
> Dr. Bob Chope (Psychologist and development expert)

LESSON 32:
Don't Swing Hard When a Soft Touch is Needed

There's a cliché that says, "If you're holding a hammer, the whole world looks like a nail." To use a sports analogy, if you're a power hitter in baseball, or a long driver in golf, it's hard not to "swing for the fences" on every shot, since the power of your swing is one of your greatest strengths on the course or ballfield. The thing is, using your strength or power on every shot rarely leads to the best outcome. This is something that I've figured out over the years, through painful experience.

This has many different applications in business, in sales, and in life, of course. In my mind, I often think back to the "old school" sales guys that were mentoring me when I came up in the sales world. They were the ones that opened my eyes to it. The issue that you can create for yourself when you're trying too hard is, "You talk to yourself right into a sale. And you can also talk yourself right out of that sale, when you're pushing too hard."

Said differently, you may have proven that you can provide a solution for the customer – but then you get so pushy with it that you turn the customer off and you end up losing the sale because you're just trying too hard.

This is similar to a 100-yard shot on the golf course. You don't need to swing as hard as you can to make this shot, as the green (target) is relatively close. This is compared to a long, 400-yard shot from the tee, where you have to use all your strength to drive the ball down the fairway as far as it will go – way before you get anywhere close to the green.

When you're close to the target, sometimes, you just have to use a soft touch to get the ball (or sale) where it needs to go. In times like this when you're close, you often need more "touch" than power. If you swing from your heels, you're likely to "overshoot" the target, one mistake may compound another, and it may take you several more shots before you get back into range to score.

In sales, the stakes are even higher – because, by "overshooting" (i.e., coming on too strong), you may wreck the trust and rapport that you've built to that point, and sometimes you can never get that back, no matter what you do.

"Don't celebrate closing a sale; celebrate opening a relationship."
Patricia Fripp (Keynote speaker and executive speech coach, 2000s)

LESSON 33:
Don't Sell Past the Close

Like the lesson above about not overshooting the green, there is a classic sales adage that says, "Don't sell past the close." This is a cliché for a reason – because it's *true*.

This was a problem for me early in my career when I was sometimes so anxious to get the sale and so competitive that I probably cost myself several sales by pushing too hard after the client was ready to buy. It seems odd to imagine, but instead of just "shutting up" and having them sign on the dotted line (as they indicated they were ready to do), I wanted to prove how much I knew and kept selling them on the features and benefits of the product.   This made the client anxious and overwhelmed. Sometimes they signed anyway – but sometimes, they didn't. And it was completely my fault each time.

One example that comes to mind happened during my time with the industrial company. I used to work with a great engineer there who loved to come out on sales calls with us. He was a prime example of being "too much." He was a very bright guy, had a wealth of knowledge about the products and our company, and was as earnest and enthusiastic as he could be. The problem came in, though, when you saw that he'd given the customer so much information that, at some point, it became too much (kind of like when the menu at a New Jersey diner or The Cheesecake Factory menu is so big that you just can't decide what to order).

Once I caught on to the pattern with this engineer, my job became reeling him in before he shared so much information that he turned the customer off.   I know that when somebody's trying to sell me something, if they get too pushy with me – especially after I've said, "Great. Where do I sign?" -- it's a huge turn off. I shut down and end up not buying anything, even if I walked into the store wanting to buy a specific item.

So, yes – you can have too much of a good thing. Sometimes "less is more" in sales, and in life!

82 | SALES IS A RELATIONSHIP

> *"Self-discipline is the bridge between goals and accomplishment."*
> *Jim Rohn (Author, entrepreneur, motivational speaker, 1990s)*

LESSON 34:
Good Things Come with Self-Discipline

Sometimes I'll be lucky enough – for a variety of reasons – to make a sale on a first visit. However, more commonly, it takes multiple meetings to go through the whole "sales cycle" to get the customer to the place where they're ready to buy. This is where patience and self-discipline come into play. They say that "patience is a virtue" – and nothing could be truer.

As we've seen throughout this book, a huge part of the sale is the relationship aspect. If you're pushing too hard, that can ruin the relationship very quickly. You have to be patient. That doesn't mean that quick sales aren't going to happen. Quick sales happen all the time, but you have to work at the speed of who you're dealing with. Some people like to get things done really quickly. Some people like to take their time.

For example, if you're dealing with a very analytical person, you probably need to slow down and take time to make sure that they're understanding all the information that you're giving them. If you walk in with a cookie cutter "quick pitch" and nothing else – if you can't take the time to get them comfortable, sticking with them until you've answered all their questions and concerns – it's probably not going to work. The customer will see that you're impatient and it will feel like you're not listening to their concerns, in which case you're wrecking rapport and trust instead of building it. And then, you're doomed.

❖ ❖ ❖ ❖ ❖ ❖ ❖

"You can observe a lot by watching."
Yogi Berra (Hall of Fame baseball player, 1960s)

LESSON 35:
Learning to Read the Room

Several of the lessons in this book – including the last several – focus on the "soft skills" that are so crucial to succeeding in sales. This lesson about "reading the room" continues that same theme.

Whether you're in an initial meet-and-greet, a final presentation, or something in-between, you have to learn to quickly assess your audience. What is their mood? How much do they know and care about your products? And, what do they want to get out of this interaction (hopefully something other than wishing you would stop talking so that they can get on with their day).

Reading the room isn't something that comes easily in my opinion. For most of us, it takes years to learn this from painful experience. You have to know how to read the *group* as well as read the *individual,* especially the key decision-maker. Then, in an instant, you have to decide how to deliver the message the best way that they (the group and the individuals in it) are going to receive it.

There are many ways to approach this. One is to break things down in your mind by the type of people that you're interacting with based on the verbal and non-verbal "cues" that they're giving off, or by their position or temperament. For example:

- If you're meeting with a highly extroverted person, the fewer the details, the better, as they are often "big picture" and "relationship"-focused. They want to know if they like and trust you -- it's all built on relationships for them – and too many facts and figures are just going to get in the way, from their perspective.

- If you're meeting with an operations leader, practical facts are likely to win the day – i.e., how are we going to implement this, what are the potholes you've seen, and how can we avoid potential landmines, risks, and disruptions?

- If you're meeting with the CFO, after some very brief pleasantries, they likely want to dive into the numbers and make sure that the details all add up. Helping them anticipate the true costs, cashflows, and collateral expenses will be expected (and appreciated, when done well).

- If you're meeting with the HR Director, they're probably most interested in how the benefits plans you're recommending are going to affect the employees and their families – balanced with concerns as to whether they can effectively argue for the increased costs as benefiting the company in the long run.

- Most other business leaders will be somewhere in between these extremes.

The quicker you can understand the information needs and communication preferences of those in the room and those making the buying decisions, the more likely you will be to walk away with a sale that is well-positioned to turn into a long-term customer relationship.

❖ ❖ ❖ ❖ ❖ ❖ ❖

> *"Sales is not about selling anymore but about building trust and educating."*
> Siva Devaki (Entrepreneur and CRM Expert, 2010s)

LESSON 36:
Taking the Time to Get Leaders Comfortable

I have an example of a client relationship from the past that touches on several of the lessons that we've been discussing – including pacing, touch, and education (i.e., knowing how fast to go, how hard to push, and how to get the team comfortable with what you're offering). Often, all these aspects need to come together in the right balance to gain the sale and cement the relationship.

In this situation, I developed a friendly personal relationship with someone before they became a customer. In casual conversations, they had complained to me a few times about the health insurance at their company. I don't like to be the "pushy" salesperson, especially with people that I have personal relationships with. They knew I handled health insurance benefits – so, I figured they would call me in for advice if they ever felt they needed it (i.e., he knew where to reach me if he needed anything). Several months after we originally met, my new friend asked me to come in and take a look at how they were handling their benefits -- and I had the opening I needed.

Given all the background that he had previously shared with me, I analyzed the situation and I went to our first official meeting very well prepared. I had put together a solution that had everything they needed. When I showed it to my friend and his leadership team, I admit that I rushed through it quickly because I was sure that I had the right answer for them. They were thrilled with what I presented and signed on the dotted line right away. It was a win-win – or so it looked at the time.

Fast-forward to a year after they had signed on with me. At that time, they were struggling to understand what was going on with their benefits plan. Not to get lost in the details, but what I had set them up with wasn't a traditional health insurance structure. It was a reimbursement setup that was relatively new and advanced at the time, but which has become much more common and well-accepted in the intervening years.

Unfortunately, I hadn't taken the time to get leadership fully up-to-speed on the details. Having hit a few bumps in the row, the executives realized that they didn't understand the plan – and most importantly, they didn't like the feel of it, especially since it had cost them a good bit of cash in that particular year.

This expense wasn't unexpected in the early years of the plan, due to its long-term design. However, the panicked looks on their faces quickly made me realize my grave mistake of not involving them nearly enough when first proposing the plan, which ultimately proved fatal.

Ironically, the new plan was actually working exactly as I had expected – and, if kept in place, it would have saved them considerable amounts in the coming years. However, because I hadn't done my job explaining it to them sufficiently in advance, it ended up costing me the customer. They felt they were misled – or, at best, that I was just another fast-talking benefits monger who promised way more than he could deliver.

This was a tough pill to swallow because I knew my plan was right and I knew that it was working. I just didn't take the time to explain it and get them comfortable – and, in the end, that made all the difference in the world, unfortunately for all of us.

❖   ❖   ❖   ❖   ❖   ❖   ❖

***"It is not enough to be compassionate —
you must act."***
Dalai Lama XIV (Tibetan spiritual leader, 1999)

LESSON 37:
Letting Someone Go As an Act of Kindness

As anyone who has ever managed people before will tell you, letting someone go is probably my least favorite thing on Earth to do. Among other issues, there is the guilt you have about affecting someone's life and livelihood so dramatically – including the impact on their family. Thankfully, for most of my career I haven't been the final decision-maker regarding a termination.

For most of my career, I was often asked to comment on someone's performance – however, the actual decision about whether to reward, retain, or dismiss the person was made by someone above my pay grade. I'm sure that some of those recommendations probably led to terminations, but I wasn't responsible for making the final call, which was a relief.

In all cases, I always tried to answer as honestly and fairly as I could, which was my responsibility to the organization, of course. I don't say this to shirk any responsibility, but rather to point out the toll a firing takes on everyone involved.

It is a fact of life in virtually all organizations that terminations occur from time to time. Now, as a business owner myself, it is likely something that I'll need to face at some point in the future – whether due to poor performance, or someone (through no fault of their own), just not being a good fit with the company and its direction at that point in time.

When it has been necessary in the past, I've tried to reflect on something a very wise person shared with me many years ago. They asked me, "Do you think that person is happy doing what they're doing?"

I said, "No."

They went on, "I agree. Clearly, they're not happy. No one wants to do a bad job. Sometimes people just get stuck in the wrong position and they can't get out. When this is the case, you're doing them a favor by letting them go, even though it's hard to see at first.

"To leave somebody in a job where they're unhappy and performing poorly, you're just going to create a bigger problem that's going to grow over the years. By letting them go, you're actually setting them up to do something that they're good at and passionate about.

It's not going to feel like it's a good thing – to either you or them -- when you have to say the words. But the truth is, keeping them "stuck" longer isn't helping anyone – not them, not the company, not yourself as their manager, and not their team."

He was right, of course – but that never makes it easier.

> *"You don't close a sale, you open a relationship if you want to build a long-term, successful enterprise."*
> Patricia Fripp (Sales Coach and Speaker, 1980s)

LESSON 38:
Maintaining Long-Term Relationships

I'm proud that some of my old customers with the industrial company followed me into the insurance world, which was extremely nice and very loyal of them. I hope that means that I proved myself to them, to where they trusted me enough to go with me in a completely different industry.

More than anything, I think this reinforces the idea that relationships are the lifeblood of sales. If you treat people right, care about their needs, show up consistently, and deliver results for them, you're going to do fine in whatever industry you choose.

Building a Book of Business from Scratch -- If we broaden our focus a little more, I'd like to share a few thoughts on "building a book" of business from scratch – which is something I had to do once I moved into the insurance world.

In the early days of my career in the industrial company (before the internet and social media came into being), the sales process literally began with the Yellow Pages and a phone. When I was a new salesperson, I would grab the phone book and start figuring out who's who – i.e., who works in the part of the industrial/distribution world we operated in, who is at the decision-making level that we need them to be, and how do I reach them (by phone or in-person)?

I repeated that process for every market, region, territory, or product segment that I was assigned to. From that point forward, it was all about knocking on doors, making countless phone calls, learning names and faces, following up, and doing it over and over again. It wasn't glamorous, but it was vital to expanding my book (and thus, my commission base).

Name Recognition -- While I was with the industrial company, we had the luxury of strong name recognition. We were a big name in the industry and had a lot of existing customers, which was a great starting point. This meant that the company name proceeded me, so I didn't need to spend time and energy introducing prospective customers to who we were and what we offered – they already knew. Therefore, I could focus a lot more on explaining the features and benefits of our products.

Transitioning to the insurance side of things, I had to start at a different point. The sales process is generally the same – albeit we now have the internet and social media as an endless source of information. The main difference was that at first, as a small start-up, we didn't have name recognition in the insurance industry. No matter – it just motivated me to work that much harder (and smarter) to get the word out about who we were, what we did, and what we could bring to potential clients.

Local Events – Starting from the ground up in the insurance world – both at my prior company and now in my own firm – I regularly participated in several "Chamber of Commerce" type of groups and local events to get our name known in the community. In addition, I do a lot of personal networking, particularly with local bankers, real estate agents and other executive level people who have set up a lot of really good networking groups.

Word of Mouth -- I've been very fortunate over the years to get a high number of "word of mouth" referrals from customers. A referral is always the best recommendation that any business can receive, from an authenticity and trustworthiness standpoint. For example, there's nothing better than when I get a call or a message that begins something like, "Bob Smith was very satisfied with your work. When he heard that I was looking for such-and-such, he recommended that I speak with you first."

All things being equal, if I can't close a sale that begins with a recommendation like that – well, it's time to hang up my spikes and retire permanently to a swing on my back porch.

❖ ❖ ❖ ❖ ❖ ❖ ❖

"Approach each customer with the idea of helping them solve a problem or achieve a goal, not selling a product or service."
Brian Tracy (Sales Trainer and Author, 1980s)

LESSON 39:
Building Trust by Solving Problems

If sales is all about the relationship, there's no better way to build a relationship than by solving someone's problem. Doing so engenders gratitude and often creates lifelong bonds – helping you do well by doing good. I believe that most who genuinely thrive in sales and entrepreneurship tend to embody this philosophy and truly take it to heart.

As you've heard me remark several times by now, I was very lucky that the first organization that I was working with had a lot of old school sales guys. When people hear that term, they tend to think of bulldog sales guys – i.e., a super gregarious, cigar smoking, pat you on the back, loudest guys in the room type of person. But I don't mean that at all when I call them "old school."

On the contrary, those guys taught me that you have two ears and one mouth and you should act accordingly. You need to listen to your customers, and you need to be reactive and proactive in helping them fix these problems. You need to fix the issues that they have going on and you also need to have the foresight to see problems that could be coming in the future. It's a lot more listening and a lot less talking in the sales game, as far as I'm concerned.

For example, let's say that you know your client has had a temporary decline in their business, cash is very tight, and they're trying very hard not to lay off anyone. When it comes time for their annual benefits renewal, they let you know upfront that anything above a 10% increase could be catastrophic for them. What do you do?

Action, Not Lip Service -- It's one thing to commiserate with customers about an upcoming increase in their medical premiums – and then go out and offer them the same 15% increase that every other broker is offering them. It rings hollow and inauthentic to tell them your "hands were tied" and you just couldn't get any concessions from the carriers -- knowing that you didn't really try to negotiate rate decreases in any meaningful way, but you happily cashed their commission check just the same.

It's quite another thing to buckle down, gather your internal brain trust, brainstorm all the different ways you could structure their benefits program this year, negotiate as aggressively as you could with the carriers, and come back to the customer with an innovative plan structure and an 8% increase – still high, of course, but one that saves them tens of thousands of dollars that year and, most importantly, likely solves a number of jobs at the company.

A customer might give you the benefit of the doubt one time, believing that "there was nothing you could do" about the increase. However, over the course of time, they'll know if you're really putting in the effort, or not. The more that you can go all out – every year and in every way – to solve their problems to the best of your ability – they'll intuitively sense that you're really trying to help them, and you'll keep them as a customer for a long, long time.

That's what it's all about!

❖   ❖   ❖   ❖   ❖   ❖   ❖

"If you 're not taking care of your customer, your competitor will."
Bob Hooey (Sales Speaker, 1990s)

LESSON 40:
Being the One Who Cares the Most

Technically, my new firm -- Shea Insurance Group – is a "new business," in that we started operations in the Spring of 2025. However, we're not really a "new" business in the traditional sense of "just starting out."

Several of us have worked together before for many years and each of us has decades of experience in our respective areas of expertise within commercial insurance, employee benefits, and administration. For those reasons, I like to think of us as a veteran crew, eager to serve our customers with the benefits of experience as well as innovative solutions for today and years to come.

Prospective customers will often ask what separates us from other independent agencies – which is exactly the right question for them to be asking, of course. There are a lot of people that sell insurance, especially in the Chicago area. Anyone switching from their current broker wants to know what they would be getting with us that's different and how we could service them better.

For that reason, I believe that getting to know us and our capabilities – and us getting to know them and their needs – is critical.

In many ways, insurance is a "commodity" product – you can get the same insurance products from a range of brokers. The difference is the service and commitment we provide. My commitment to them is that no one will care more about their needs or work harder to meet their needs to the fullest extent possible.

Part of this is finding a broker where you're in their "sweet spot," and vice-versa. We work a lot in the small and midsize business arena. That's a really good market for us. In the Chicagoland area, there are a lot of huge brokerage firms that like to target the very large companies. That's fine. They can probably service them better than we can. So, we try to stick to those customers that fall into the arena where we know we can be really helpful. We're very well-equipped to support small and mid-size organizations, so that's where we focus our attention.

"I have not failed. I've just found 10,000 ways that won't work."
Thomas Edison (Inventor, founder of General Electric)

LESSON 41:
Using Humor to Good Effect

Before we enter the home stretch (or the "back nine," to continue our ongoing golf analogy) of more serious lessons learned, I wanted to sprinkle in another "lighter" (but still important) tip. This has to do with using humor in presentations.

They say that "The best-laid plans sometimes go awry." In my experience, nowhere is this more true than in group presentations. When things start going wrong in a meeting or presentation, my go-to is to try to use gentle humor – even better if it's self-deprecating. A specific example is a presentation I gave for a large group of close to one thousand people in Texas when was I with the industrial company.

When you're traveling, you don't always have everything that you need with you. In this case, as I was packing, I grabbed the wrong suit. Those who know me know that my weight can fluctuate by a fair number of pounds up or down at any given time. (For better or worse, I can lose or gain weight fairly quickly). For that reason, I keep several different size suits in my closet at all times.

This time, I grabbed a suit where the pants were definitely a little bit too small for me. Predictably, at some point on my way to the stage, I split my pants. "There's nothing new under the sun," I know, and this has happened to millions of people over the years – but still, it was embarrassing. Happily, nobody else knew about this at the time, but me. However, if you're not stressed enough walking onto a stage in front of close to a thousand people, try doing so knowing that there's a big split in the back of your pants. It is something to experience!

In any case, things were going well – until, at some point in my talk, I moved to the side, exposing the split from a certain angle. I could see that a few people noticed it, and I started seeing some laughs while the rest of the room didn't know what was going on.

You could see maybe a third of the room had caught it. So, finally, about two minutes after that, I decided to just go ahead and turn around and admit my misfortune, and it got a huge laugh.

There were a lot more friendly laughs after that one, since now everyone was "in" on the joke – so, it felt like everyone was laughing *with* me rather than *at* me. I think having the ability and the willingness to publicly "make fun" of myself went a long way in building trust and human connection with a room full of people that you I didn't know.

Like the quote from Thomas Edison, above, I've found that life (and sales) goes a lot easier if you have a sense of humor and a sense of humility. We all have our pride, of course – but if we can't laugh at ourselves, I believe we're taking life a little too seriously. That's my story and I'm sticking to it!

> ***"Nobody cares how much you know, until they know how much you care."***
> Theodore Roosevelt (U.S. President, early 1900s)

LESSON 42:
Empathy Diffuses Anger

For most of us, public speaking is nerve-wracking on the best day, even if you're experienced. It is an even more difficult task to accomplish well when you have a difficult, hostile, skeptical, uninterested, or even confrontational audience. I've been lucky to not have any major failures in ESSthis regard – but I've certainly been in my fair share of "challenging" situations. Most often, I've found that showing empathy works best in getting a skeptical crowd onto your side.

In the health insurance world, 90-percent of the audience in the obligatory annual benefits meetings is just trying to get through the meeting, making their selections, and get back to their desk as quickly as possible. Then you have 10-percent of the people that have had issues with health insurance, whether it was claims, denials, or big bills – which is where the challenging questions and concerns come from.

When an unhappy person comes into that room, you can sense it right away. Sometimes you don't even have to be particularly sensitive to pick this up – they often announce their concerns to you and the room loudly and in no uncertain terms, right from the start. I've learned that being empathetic, respectful, and non-defensive is the key to lowering the level of emotion in the room and having productive exchanges with the upset employee.

In these situations, it's a balance, because you can't "cater" to them at the expense of the rest of the audience, of course. But, you have to take at least a few moments to show empathy towards them and really listen to their issues and try to talk them through it. If you don't neutralize the disruption, it can spin out of control and you can lose the entire room, which helps no one.

If you can find common ground and identify where the issue began – e.g., if a provider made a mistake, or if there was a coding error, or if they misunderstood the plan that they were on, or something along those lines – then, you generally, you can find a resolution or at least a pathway to solve the problem that they're having.

It takes patience – but this will often calm the situation enough so that you can move on with the presentation and help the person resolve the issue more fully afterward. If you authentically care about resolving their issue, they'll sense this and almost always meet you half-way. Once you're solving the problem together, it's usually an easy leap from skepticism to trust – and that makes all the difference in the world.

❖ ❖ ❖ ❖ ❖ ❖ ❖

"Stop selling. Start helping."
Zig Ziglar (Sales guru and motivational speaker, 1980s)

LESSON 43:
Helping Leaders Help Themselves

If sales is really all about building trusting relationships, then there's nothing more meaningful and lasting we can do than to help business owners help themselves and their employees through expert advice and wise counsel. Here are a few ways that I've seen this play out, time and time again.

The popular narrative is sometimes that business owners are greedy, out for themselves, and don't look out for their employees. My experience over the past 25+ years is quite the contrary. You always get a bad penny from time to time, but for the most part, business owners are trying to do everything they can to keep as many people happy as possible, while providing livelihoods for them.

It's true that the business owner sometimes gets rewarded quite handsomely for his labor -- but that usually comes years later. For those companies that are in their first five to ten years, often that owner isn't taking a salary or is taking a lot less money than he or she was accustomed to before starting their business.

Sometimes, we'll see an employer that's trying to be "too generous" to employees, maybe more so than they can afford. At those times, my job (at least in terms of formulating their benefits plans) becomes gently reminding the owner that if they don't have money to keep their doors open, none of their employees will have jobs or health insurance – thus, helping no one. In my experience, many business owners are extremely kind and generous to their employees and sometimes you have to protect them from themselves, so to speak.

Other times, you have to help them see into the future and anticipate future costs, trends, and risks. Again, not to get too lost in the health insurance details, but my conversation with the owner and leadership team might sound like the following:

"Hey, you're on a fully funded right now, and that's worked very well for you. Your premiums and risks have been very stable, which is great. Looking a little further down the line, though, we need to take a serious look at self-insurance this year, because I think you're leaving half a million dollars on the table by sticking with a fully funded plan instead of becoming self-insured. That half million dollars would allow you to provide better plans at better rates for your employees."

You have to have a sympathetic attitude and fully understand what ownership is going through and what their outlook is -- not only over the next 12 months, but over the next five years. From there, you try to structure a plan that's going to work for them for the long haul. Sometimes that means becoming self-insured; sometimes it might mean using other funding or risk-control vehicles.

Regardless of the answer, the point is that it's my job to help the owner look to the future, to protect everyone concerned as best is possible. By doing so, I'm building trust between us and hopefully setting up a strong relationship for many years to come.

❖   ❖   ❖   ❖   ❖   ❖   ❖

"The secret of selling anything is to find out what the other person wants and help them get it."
Frank Bettger (Author, *How I Raised Myself from Failure to Success in Selling*, 1947)

LESSON 44:
Keeping the Peace in Difficult Meetings

Earlier in the book, we talked a little about how to read the room and customize your "pitch" depending on the needs and preferred styles of the leadership team. I wanted to expand on that thought by considering additional strategies for resolving other customer conflicts that occur within meetings and presentations. Sometimes, you have to play salesperson, psychologist, peacemaker, and advisor, all at the same time.

People on Different Pages -- I once had a customer where every time I walked into a meeting with the leadership team, everybody had a very different opinion. It made me wonder, "Don't they talk about this stuff together except when I'm here?" – which turned out to be a legitimate question. Everyone was definitely on a different page from everyone else.

They were very good customers, but it was a very uncomfortable room to walk in, especially I knew I was walking into the same thing every year and nothing (and no one) seemed to ever change. Every year we got through the meeting relatively unscathed, but it was always very trying. I certainly felt like I earned my commission (and "hazardous duty pay") just by helping the owner survive the meeting.

In the meeting, you want to listen to everybody, and you want to try to address as many of the concerns as possible. At the same time, you can't be afraid to challenge people, either, because a lot of times things will be said that are incorrect. No one else in the room is going to know the plans and the numbers as well as you do. This is where your expertise as well as your interpersonal skills are most needed.

You can't be afraid to voice your opinion, diplomatically but confidently, of course. Occasionally, doing so may get you thrown out and you may lose the sale – but, you'll keep your integrity, knowing that you've given them the best advice and information possible. Usually, though, the group will take your lead and some type of compromise solution will be found.

I wanted to mention here one other unique situation I experienced in the past – which might be "the exception that proves the rule":

One of my customers was a very successful company where the founder was now approaching retirement age. He had three family members who were in the process of taking over the company in the coming years and he was trying to make this happen in an organized and peaceful way. Suffice to say, as in any situation where there are money, power, and legacies involved, there were lots of family "dynamics" to navigate in that situation.

Family Therapy -- I've never seen this before anywhere else, but the founder made his heirs go to weekly therapy sessions – together! -- to deal with any problems they may have had with each other. Talk about "thinking outside the box" in approaching difficult situations in creative ways.

When I walked into the room for our annual benefits review meeting with the leadership team, those folks truly knew each other's feelings, needs, and perspectives about a range of company issues, including the benefits plans. I don't know how they all get along at Thanksgiving dinner or holiday get togethers – but I can tell you that was a surprisingly comfortable room to be in each year.

At the very least, everything was out in the open and we could work through the issues in an objective and unemotional way. (Hats off to the counselor, who clearly had done her job well). I wish all my meetings with leadership teams were like that!

"To be yourself in a world that is constantly trying to make you something else is the greatest accomplishment."
Ralph Waldo Emerson (American writer, 1841)

LESSON 45
Being the Same Person at all Times

"Being the same person no matter where you go" is something I've talked with my kids about a lot. I believe it's a tough thing to do for most of us – so, when someone really is "always the same," I feel that it's a compliment to them.

Over the years, I've had a lot of people that were either friends and then became customers -- or were customers and then became friends – so, I've had a lot of crossover between my personal and professional lives. Sometimes it can get a little tricky to know where boundaries are when someone moves from one side to the other. One of the compliments I've received that I'm most proud of is hearing someone who knows both "sides" of me say that I'm the "same person" whether I'm working, or whether we're at a bar or in a Cubs game, or wherever we might be. I try hard to always be that "same person" that acts and treats people the same way, regardless of anything else.

The part that I try to particularly emphasize to my kids is for them to be whoever their true self is. If they treat people the same kind and friendly way -- whether they're playing sports, or at school, or in the neighborhood – then I feel like I've done my part as a parent, at least in this aspect of parenting.

Certainly, you're going to be more comfortable with family and friends than you're going to be with customers. But you can be the same genuine person. If people know that they can count on you showing up as the same person wherever you are, I think that's important. I think it helps people have a level of comfort with you when they know what they're getting. If someone can say to me, "Hey, I bet you're the same guy when you're doing the presentation in front of my 50 employees as you are having a chat and a beer on the 19th hole of the golf course," that means a lot to me – and I think it helps build the relationship for the long haul.

❖   ❖   ❖   ❖   ❖   ❖   ❖

> *"When the trust account is high, communication is easy, instant, and effective."*
> Stephen R. Covey (Management guru and author, *The Seven Habits of Highly Effective People*)

LESSON 46:
Due Diligence Builds Trust

When you hear someone say that they "did their due diligence," it often brings to minds of lawyers, accountants, and other technical experts checking out an organization or individual. Put in more down-to-earth terms, someone might say that they "vouch" for someone else. Whatever we call it, this process is important for building a trusting relationship with your customer. Here's what I mean.

On the employee benefits side of our business, just about any broker can get access to any insurance carrier. That doesn't mean that all carriers are the same, though. Part of what you're paying your broker for is for them to guide you to only use reputable vendors that meet your needs. Trust is built when you see your broker looking out for your best interests – and as a customer, you can rest much easier at night when this is the case.

This requires me as your broker to stay up to date with the latest goings on in the insurance industry, in order to share with you the best recommendations possible. For example, if you see that a carrier is struggling for one reason or another, you have to look out for your clients' interests and keep them posted if things start happening that they should be aware of – especially if a change to another carrier is potentially called for. You have to use all available information to the client's advantage, which compels you to keep up with everything going on in the industry.

On the commercial side of things, meeting with carrier representatives is something that I've always done. And, I always ask them the same questions, like "What are you good at, and what are you not good at what? What kind of business do you want to take on?" Their answers let me know if I feel comfortable placing my client's trust in them, and if we're a good fit.

For example, I'm always looking out for who wants to ensure my roofers and my cement guys and my truck drivers and the trades that nobody else wants. Having open dialogues with them is the job of the broker, and I take pride in it. It not only builds trust with the client when I recommend a top-notch carrier to them, but it also reinforces the idea that I have my pulse on the industry, and I know where to steer them and where not to steer them.

None of my clients are experts in insurance – and it's very hard for them to differentiate between "OK" carriers and "great" carriers who truly meet their needs. That's what I'm there for, to advise them. By keeping an open dialogue between me, the broker, and the carrier, I can avoid putting customers with carriers who don't want to write their business or aren't good at it. At the end of the day, it's my reputation – and the trust relationship that I've built with the customer – that's on the line.

I wouldn't have it any other way!

❖   ❖   ❖   ❖   ❖   ❖   ❖

"The best salespeople know it's not about selling — it's about solving."
Unknown (Sales Adage, late 20th century)

LESSON 47:
Spurring Out of the Box Thinking

As I learned early on during my days as a young industrial salesperson, a good bit of my job involves trying to come up with "out of the box" solutions to solve customer problems. I wanted to touch on this further, sharing how this has applied to my work in the insurance industry. I've found that offering solutions that not every other broker brings to the table builds trust and confidence, as well as sales.

For example, in the health insurance industry, there really aren't "negotiations" with carriers in the same way that there used to be. These days, they give you a price based on ACA (Affordable Care Act, aka "Obamacare") guidelines, and your customer's employee census and past healthcare usage. In this way, carriers move pretty quickly from "How old are they (the employees of your customer)?" to "Where are they located?" to "OK --here's your price."

The truth is that, by and large, every broker's going to get the same rates – i.e., if we give the carrier the exact same employee census data, we're all going to get the exact same price. Knowing this, we have to start asking ourselves how we can put things together in an "outside the box" way that gives our customer an advantage – i.e., out of the 40 to 80 plan options that we have with Cigna, Aetna, United Healthcare, etc., what can we build that's going to be different and going to bring the most bang for the buck to our customer?

Like many other things in life, there usually aren't any shortcuts to success in this regard -- you have to go through the details. Sometimes, you almost have to take on the role of an actuary, recognizing that this plan has a lower OOPM (Out of Pocket Maximum) than this other one, but it still has a cheaper premium. Why is it that? The answer might be that the insurance carrier wants to push people to a particular network, or to a particular deductible level to share risks – or any other strategy that might become apparent by looking at the details.

There are a thousand different ways to go with different combinations and scenarios, which is where a broker's expertise comes into play. It is exactly that unique vision and expertise that we're "selling" to customers.

❖   ❖   ❖   ❖   ❖   ❖   ❖

> *"A satisfied customer is the best business strategy of all."*
> Michael LeBoeuf (Author, *How to Win Customers and Keep Them for Life*)

LESSON 48:
Negotiating Well Without Getting Greedy

One of the key parts of my job that I've always found invigorating is negotiations -- I find them fun, really. While these discussions in the insurance industry aren't nearly as wide-open as in other fields, I still enjoy the back-and-forth of a good, respectful negotiation. I think that that's part of my competitive nature. I like feeling like I came out on top and achieved my objectives in some way.

Most often, negotiations aren't total victories for either side. However, even a partial win gives me a rush – so that I can go to sleep that night knowing that I won something for my customers. If I can follow up with a customer and let them know something like, "Your premium on this was $112, 000. We got it down to $98, 000" when they weren't expecting that – well, that's a very good day, for sure.

On the other side of the transaction, the carrier might be laughing, thinking, "We would have done it for $80,000." That's ok if we all win. As they say on Wall Street, "Bulls make money. Bears make money. Pigs get slaughtered." There's no reason to get greedy. Arriving at a fair resolution gives us the ability to go back to the same carrier next year and negotiate where the vendor knows that we're reasonable to work with, and the client knows that we're looking out for their best interests. We can call that a "win – win – win."

I love almost all parts of my job. I have to say, the feeling of solving a problem for a customer -- that's probably the best feeling. But winning negotiations are pretty dang good feelings, too.

Learning Negotiations at the Poker Table – I wanted to share one other story with you from my past, to bring to life the "negotiations" idea more vividly. This goes all the way back to my childhood, growing up in a suburb of Chicago.

I've always enjoyed playing poker for as long as I can remember. I can't say that I'm "good" at it, because I don't play it nearly enough -- but I grew up playing with my grandma that lived with us. She taught me at a very young age, and would I play with my dad's buddy sometimes, and we had some neighborhood games going on, too.

One of the guys that was always in our neighborhood games had actually won a World Series of Poker bracelet, and he wasn't shy about mentioning this fact. So, he would walk in every week and just have a bullseye on his back, where we'd be playing the best cards against him, just so we could say that we beat him -- but we all still had fun with it.

I find that poker is really one big "negotiation" of bidding, bluffing, and trying to anticipate your opponent's next move, so that you can ultimately bring the game to a conclusion. The difference between poker and business, though, is that in poker, you're just trying to win the pot – you're not trying to build long-term friendships with your fellow players, necessarily.

In business, it never pays to get greedy (as we noted above) by taking everything off the table at the same time. If you do that, you might "win the battle" (i.e., get the customer to sign for a deal that's heavily weighted to your side because they have no other options at the moment), but you'll always lose the war (i.e., lose the customer once they figure out they're being taken advantage of and they really do have other options out there).

It's much better, I believe, if everyone comes out of the negotiation feeling that their concerns have been heard and they got at least a partial "win" out of the deal.

❖ ❖ ❖ ❖ ❖ ❖ ❖

"In any moment of decision, the best thing you can do is the right thing."
Theodore Roosevelt (U.S. President, 1904)

LESSON 49:
Doing Right and Setting an Example

All of us come upon moral dilemmas from time to time – whether in business, or sales, or life in general. I've certainly been in business situations that have made me uncomfortable – but luckily those have been very few and far between. I wanted to share a few thoughts on this with you, though.

From a business or sales standpoint, frankly, I think these situations are simple – but not easy -- to navigate, if you have a solid moral background. I came from an Irish Catholic Family and morality was very, very important to both my mom and dad. They sent us to schools that promoted strong ethics and morality above everything else. And I'd like to think that I carried a lot of that with me into my professional career.

It's not something I talk about a lot, to be honest with you, but it is something that's extremely important to me – especially raising two kids right now that are currently 14 and 12. It's important for me to set an example, and it's come up a few times over the course of my professional career.

Surrounding yourself with good people -- One thing we were talking about with our kids was making sure that you surround yourself with good people. I always say that if you think somebody has different values than you, it doesn't mean you can't be nice to them and talk to them. You should absolutely be nice and talk to them. But as far as the people that you're going to choose to spend your time with, they should be good people that have similar moral beliefs, goals, and desires in life. It's much easier to stay on the right track if you have like-minded friends, family, and colleagues beside you.

Being True to Yourself -- In one of my more recent life decisions, I found myself to be preaching about "being true to yourself" to my kids and then wondering if I was living up to my own words. It's like, how can I be preaching this if I'm not doing this myself?

Luckily, I haven't had a million of those moral conundrums, but enough where decisions had to be made that that sometimes can be very scary decisions (financially and otherwise) -- but where I have to do what I think is right. Period.

It helped a great deal talking this out with my wife and kids. Once I heard myself say the words, I was able to see the answer clearly, and the decision was easy.

My Dad's Example -- Going back to another example set by my dad, I once talked with him about why he switched companies once when I was a kid. He did that because he felt that was the moral move. He was in a management position, and the company wanted him to fire somebody. He felt that this was wrong for a number or reasons. His feeling was 180 degrees from the company's view. He knew the person had value and he didn't agree with the reasons that they wanted to terminate them. He ended up resigning because he refused to fire that person.

Seeing that happen had a big impact on me when I was very young, and even more so when I understood it more deeply later in life. Seeing people make decisions based on their moral compass leaves a lasting impression. I'm not a perfect person, of course -- and I've made my more than my fair share mistakes. However, remembering where you come from and remembering the Golden Rule of right and wrong is the key.

Whether it's in business or life in general, the same concepts of morality apply and should be an integral part of your decision making. Whether you're an owner, worker, customer, or vendor, right is right. Regardless of whether you're selling something or choosing where you're going to work or who you're going to work for, your ethics should prevail in every decision.

This is easier said than done many times, of course. But I can only recommend it as the best way to sleep soundly at night, regardless of the decision at hand.

❖ ❖ ❖ ❖ ❖ ❖ ❖

"Timid salesmen have skinny kids."
Zig Ziglar (Sales Guru and Motivational Speaker, 1970s)

LESSON 50:
The Importance of Drive

I think it's important to have a different drive than most people if you're salesperson. You're rewarded for the work that you get done in the most literal sense – i.e, with earned commissions. So, you have to be willing to push a little harder than most – especially in roles where your commissions may far outweigh your monthly salary.

A salesperson has to be driven a little bit differently -- more aggressively – than many other roles and functions. In sales, going all out is expected and required for success. I think that's why a lot of driven people like me probably do a little bit better in sales, because we're willing to go the extra mile when it comes customer requests like, "Hey, can you do this on a Saturday or Sunday?" The answer is always, "Sure." If I can possibly do it – and if it will help me get the deal done -- I'll make it happen.

Hustle, drive, and grit are important qualities to ensure that you meet your personal performance and financial goals. However, the flip side of having exceptionally strong drive -- and I've seen it with my own eyes – is that it can cause problems in other areas of life, most typically your personal life.

The question of work-life balance in sales is a story for another time and place, though. For now, I can only encourage those with drive to "go for it" with a sales career, if they are so inclined. It has made for a very satisfying career for me and for millions of others, if this is how you're wired. Go get 'em!

❖   ❖   ❖   ❖   ❖   ❖   ❖

"Make a customer, not a sale."
Katherine Barchetti (Luxury Retailer, 1980s)

LESSON 51:
When They Count on You Personally

There's an expression that says, "Be careful what you wish for – you may get it." While this is most often said "tongue in cheek" with a wink and a smile, there is a great truth here when it comes to sales, in this way. For the entire book up until now, I've been "preaching" about the virtue and goal of building trusting relationships. When you're successful in this, it is rewarding beyond measure. It can also be very challenging from a personal perspective, when others count and depend on you.

I wouldn't trade it for the world. I would just caution you to be ready for the challenges that come your way when others depend on you. Be aware of the responsibility, accept and embrace it, and dive right in!

To illustrate this, I wanted to share kind of a scary story that involves one of my very, very good customers on both the benefits and the commercial side of business – somebody I've been working with since the very beginning of my insurance career. Here's what happened.

I received a call on either a Friday night or a Saturday morning. I don't recall exactly, but it was certainly not during work hours. My phone starts ringing, and I see the name on the phone, and there's no way I'm not answering it, because not only are they fantastic customers, but also very close friends. When I answered it, the gentleman on the other end was in a panic.

I said, "All right, calm down. What's going on?" He said, "My daughter just got hit by a car." She was five or six years old at this point. "She's in the ambulance and they're on the way to the hospital."

Trying to get the lay of the land, I asked, "Do we know anything medically at this point?" He said, "No, but it doesn't look great." There was a pause and then he said, "How do I handle this?"

What I'm thinking in my head is, "From an insurance standpoint, his medical insurance is solid. Somebody hit her with a car. We're going to figure out if that person has insurance -- but even if that person doesn't have insurance, it's going to be fine."

As he's asking rapid-fire questions from being in shock at what happened, I said, "Listen, just go to the hospital. Go be with your daughter and your wife. Make sure everything's okay there. This is all going to work out" – which is what happened. But it could have easily been much, much worse – even tragic.

Fast forward a couple of years: The girl is healthy, and everything is good, thankfully. But I had kids that were a little older at that time and I kept thinking about how unbelievably scary that has to be for a parent to go through, when you just feel completely helpless with your kid. I'm so thankful that the story has a happy ending.

Stepping back and looking at this from a broader perspective, I've had numerous calls like this from customers in the past – where I'm getting a call that doesn't really have to do with me because it's not an insurance question. It's more just like, "This bad thing happened and what the hell am I supposed to do right now?"

It sounds strange to say, but this situation – and other calls like it -- made me feel good because I realize that there has to be a certain level of trust built with you when they're calling you for help and advice under those scary circumstances. It made me feel extremely useful at that moment.

If my customers (and a lot of them have become my friends) are comfortable enough to call me in those situations, it means I built a good level of trust with them, where the business side of things becomes the easy part.

I think being genuine and honest with people in the good times and in the bad times – and taking the time to talk them through problems when they arise -- is extremely important. People are smart and intuitive. They know when someone's being genuine with them.

Authenticity and honesty both go a long way with most everybody – and it helps you put your head on the pillow each night and sleep soundly, knowing that you did your best to serve and support others.

"*Wherever you go, go with all your heart.*"
Confucius (Chinese philosopher, 5th century BC)

LESSON 52:
Getting There (Planes and Automobiles)

Throughout my career, I've always tried to go "above and beyond" for my clients. Often, this has involved being willing to travel wherever and whenever needed. Fortunately, not too many of my trips involved mishaps of the level that Steve Martin and John Candy encountered in the old movie, "Planes, Trains, and Automobiles." I've usually been able to overcome whatever obstacles arose without too much trouble. Here is one of my favorite stories in that regard.

This happened a few years ago and involved a large customer that we handled the health benefits for. In the employee benefits business, the fourth quarter is extremely chaotic because the majority of customers roll out new plans to their employees which go into effect on January 1st. We're traveling a lot and negotiating the final details of the plans up to the last minute, all while we're trying to get materials prepared for the presentations.

The Challenge -- We were having a difficult time with a few different aspects of this customer's renewal – so, everything took a bit longer than usual to come together. We finally got things done with very little time to spare before we had to meet with and enroll all 900 of their employees, spread out nationally. The team and I were staring at each other, wondering, "How are we going to get these open enrollment meetings done in time?" There were four offices in the Northeast, five offices on the West Coast, and a few more in the Midwest.

The Plan -- From my background of traveling, it's a skill that I probably take for granted. I know that some people dread traveling – especially for business – but I've always found that it's not as difficult as people think. (To be fair, my home airport is Chicago O'Hare, which has direct and non-stop flights virtually anywhere in the country – so, I admit to being spoiled).

With the number of flights that are going in and out of major cities these days, and the ease of renting cars (and now with Uber and Lyft almost everywhere), I've always been able to get where I needed to be without too much trouble. (Knock on wood, of course). So, we're looking at everything as a team, and one person said, "I can do these cities." Another guy at the firm said he could handle a few other cities, and a third could handle several other locations. I knew I could take of the rest – so, within a short while, the problem was solved.

The Complication -- There was a bit of a hang-up when I started to look at the details of getting myself from Pittsburgh to Cleveland, which aren't that far from one another but don't have a lot of convenient flights between them, for whatever reason. So, I figured that I would just rent a car. It would take five or six hours to drive, which is a lot easier than going 1000 miles out of my way with some crazy multi-leg stop-over.

How It Worked Out -- So, we scheduled the trip, I knocked out the meeting in one city, rented a car, drove all night, went to the other one, caught a couple hours of sleep, did the next, and ended up taking care of three offices in two days. Out of a 40-hour time span, I probably worked or traveled for 36 of those 40 hours -- to the point where the customer thought I was crazy.

The funny part came when the HR person looked at me and said, "Who's doing the West Coast?" Without missing a beat, I was happy to say, "I leave for the West Coast tomorrow." I went out to the West Coast and delivered presentations to the four locations there in a two-day period.

By the time that week was over, I was a little bit exhausted -- I was literally falling into a hotel bed, sleeping for a couple hours, and getting back after it. Everyone – and my wife was included in this group – was telling me, "You're absolutely nuts." The truth is, though, to me those are the really fun weeks.

I know it's not healthy for us to do this regularly -- but when you're in the middle of a sprint like this, you're so busy and you are on such a tight schedule to get everything done, it's a rush of adrenaline. If people weren't coming into the open enrollment meetings, we were walking through warehouses and dragging them in to get enrolled because we knew how tight a window we had.

What really helped was that I wasn't the only one on the team who was traveling and conducting the meetings. There were a couple other guys doing the exact same thing, and we had three people at the office backing up all the meetings – so, it was a true team effort.

We were able to get to all the offices within a matter of a few days, and it worked out fantastically. There was a lot of chaos behind the scenes, but those are the weeks that I love. It's definitely hard work, but I love being busy. And I never shy away from a good challenge.

❖   ❖   ❖   ❖   ❖   ❖   ❖

"A man who pays the bill isn't just a man,
he is a provider"
Anonymous

LESSON 53:
Always Pick Up the Tab

One of simplest but most important business lessons that I learned from my dad – that was reinforced again and again by my early mentors at the industrial company – is the importance of the salesperson picking up the tab when out with customers or prospects. This is always true, even when the customer doesn't let you pick up the tab.

Special Dinner -- I recently took the CFO of one of my large customers out to dinner. We've had the habit of having our quarterly meetings over lunch. This time, we happened to make it a dinner for various reasons – which was great, because it allowed my wife, Laura, to join us. The CFO and Laura have met several times and have become friends over the years.

We were just talking and having a good time at a very nice steakhouse that the CFO had chosen. I could tell towards the end of the dinner, she was feeling uneasy about something – which was surprising, because everyone had a wonderful meal and seemed to be relaxed and enjoying themselves.

When it was time to pack things up and get back on the road, I looked at the waiter and said, "I'll take the bill." This triggered a quick response from the CFO, who said, "No, I'll take the bill." I said, "Thank you, but you are not taking the bill. One, you're my customer. And two, I'm not letting you pick up this tab because I knew it was going to be a costly one." So, we were at a bit of a standstill.

She replied, "I actually talked to the owners of the company and the executive team this afternoon, and we decided we're buying you dinner in appreciation for all that you've done for us." To this, I said, "I'm honored, and I appreciate the gesture – but you're still not paying the bill."

I paid it, and that was that. But the back-and-forth was kind of fun because it was all coming from a good place on both sides.

Protocol -- I actually get yelled at fairly often for this by my vendors (like the insurance carriers that we work with). They always say, "Well, you know, we're supposed to be paying the tab for you, not the other way around." It's just that as a lifelong sales guy, I'm used to picking up the tabs because it's generally our job.

I thought it was very nice offer from the CFO (above) and I was touched by the gesture. However, I make a very nice amount of money doing business with her organization. They've always been extremely loyal to me and followed me over to the new company without me even having to ask the question. It might seem backwards, but in a situation where I've built such a trusting relationship with someone that they wanted to pick up a tab as a sign of appreciation – well, that one should definitely be on me.

Customers Becoming Friends – The same customer was so kind as to invite my family to one of her child's very first birthdays. I don't want to say it's a regular occurrence because it's still a special occasion when it happens. When you have the same customers for years and years, you become close with them, and you build up a level of trust both ways -- me trusting them and them, trusting me. It's nice when a friendship comes out of it.

Others may feel different, but I believe that situations like this help the business relationship. I find that a friendly relationship enables you to be more candid than normal when you have to share something important with them –

like when you feel that they're making a bad decision from an insurance perspective.

The reverse is true, too – they can be more open with me if they feel our service levels aren't where they need to be, or one of our team members isn't doing what they should be doing. It's nice to know they can reach out to me and let me know what's going on without putting the relationship at risk.

"At the root of every successful marriage is a strong partnership."
Carson Daly (Television personality and radio host)

LESSON 54:
Benefits of Marrying an Amazing Spouse

More than anything in my life, I'm grateful every day that I married the love of my life, Laura, and that we've been blessed with our two children. Full stop. There's nothing more important to me than this, for more reasons than I can possibly say.

Recently, after two decades together, our relationship has taken on another dimension, as we've been working together since founding our new firm, which has been another blessing.

Honestly, that's a testament to Laura. She's been great at everything that she's done in her career. Unlike me, who's been in sales my entire working life, she's been successful in a variety of fields. She's been a dental assistant, an EKG machine reader, and a Montessori school teacher. Most recently, she was a Catholic school teacher. She's been in several different roles, and she's been extremely successful in all of them, which has been very fortunate for me, as she picks up new skills at any amazing rate.

When I started making plans to form my own agency, I realized right away that I was going to need help – and Laura was the first and only person I thought of. Knowing that she was happy in her teaching career, I approached the topic with caution, not wanting to pull her away from something that she loved. However, I gathered the courage to get the words out and asked her, "Is this something that you're willing to do?"

Thankfully, her answer was "Yes." Being the person that she is, before I knew it, she was taking online classes to get licensed in insurance and watching webinars and YouTube videos. She was off and running learning the agency management software and the different portals that would be needed as the administrative foundation of our new operation.

After all these years, I shouldn't have been surprised – but, I was amazed at how quickly she was picking some insurance-specific things that needed to be done, like popping out certificates of insurance and other necessary details. She's extremely efficient and was keeping my customer base very happy with how responsive she was to any and all requests. Customers were emailing me, asking where did I find her, and how long has she been doing this for it? It's truly a testament to Laura, who is a wonderful person, to boot.

So, the "lesson" here is to marry a wonderful multi-talented woman. I think it's easier said than done, but if you can pull it off, it's what you want to do!

❖ ❖ ❖ ❖ ❖ ❖ ❖

> *"Earn your success based on service to others, not at the expense of others."*
> H. Jackson Brown Jr. (Author, *Life's Little Instruction Book*)

LESSON 55:
Rooting for the Little Guy and Giving Back

For the final "lesson" of this book, I wanted to share with you a little about some of the most important things to and about me – kind of a "one from the heart" message, if you will.

As a salesperson and now as a business owner, I want to serve as many customers as I can in as many industries and locations as I can serve well. So, I root for everyone – large, Fortune-500 companies; start-up tech companies; longtime mom-and-pop local businesses that have been the mainstays of their communities for decades – and everything in-between. If I can serve you well, I want you to be my customer.

There is one general type of business that is probably closest to my heart than all others. I have to admit that I find myself gravitating toward the small and mid-sized independent businesses the most, for a few reasons.

- You're not dealing with anonymous stockholders and unknown Boards of Directors and everything else that comes with large corporations.

- You're generally dealing with families or groups of friends or siblings that have put together these companies with their blood, sweat, and tears – and you know insurance and other business decisions have direct effects on their life.

- You know going in that if insurance costs go up thirty thousand dollars unexpectedly, well, that could be little Charlie's college fund or the difference between whether the owners get to retire this year or five years from now.

I've been lucky enough to work for a couple of privately held companies as my employer – and thousands more as my customers – and I think that's probably why that's where my heart belongs. I've watched those families work through a lot of that real-life stuff. I've also been blessed to be able to watch a lot of these independently owned companies do extremely well.

It's fun to watch the hard work come to fruition and to see how it has a direct effect on the owners and everyone around them. So often, when the owner is having that much success, they are happy to share it with the people that help them get there – their employees, and the community at-large. It's a great thing to see.

I don't root against anybody. I have great respect for the publicly traded companies and the people that that own their stock. I hope they make all the money in the world. I root a little bit harder, though, when it's the small and mid-sized businesses that are having success.

It's the All-American story, really. That's what I've been blessed to be, as well --so, believe me, I'm rooting for myself, too. Working hard and doing well and doing good is what it's all about.

As a final note ...

I hope that these thoughts and reflections have been helpful and interesting to you. If I can ever be of service, it would be my great pleasure. Please reach out at any time: george@sheaig.com. I look forward to speaking with you!

RECENT CUSTOMER & FAMILY PHOTOS

On the golf course with friends and our boys

Golfing with friends and customers

My daughter and I at a customer event

The Friendly Confines of Wrigley Field is a favorite venue for passing wonderful weekend afternoons with friends and customers

Supporting longtime customers at a gala event

Winning a golf event with one of my best friends

With my amazing wife, Laura, visiting customers

Kidding around and joining in the fun celebrating Halloween with a customer

Enjoying a day on the golf course with customers

And one more, for good measure, to bring us full-circle to where it all began – on the golf course.

ABOUT THE AUTHORS

George Shea

George founded Shea Insurance Group based on 20+ years of sales and leadership experience. This book distills lessons he has learned in business and life, beginning with childhood memories of summertime trips accompanying "the best salesperson he's ever seen," his dad. When he's not serving customers' commercial insurance and employee benefits needs, he can be found enjoying time with family and friends at home, on golf courses and ballfields, and in the community.

George can be reached at: george@sheaig.com .

Michael Brisciana

Michael recently stepped away from a 30+ year career in Human Resources to pursue a "second act" in writing, consulting, and other creative ventures. During his time in HR, he worked with fast-growing start-ups, non-profits, and Fortune-500 firms, always striving to help managers and employees develop to their fullest potential. He is the author of *Empathetic Leadership* and *Is It OK To Be Quiet?* and a lifelong New York sports fan.

Michael can be reached at: michael@quietkidbooks.com .

ABOUT THE SHEA INSURANCE GROUP

At Shea Insurance Group, we are dedicated to providing personalized insurance solutions tailored to meet the unique needs of each client. With years of experience in the industry, our team of experts offers a wide range of coverage options, from employee benefits to home & auto policies to life insurance and business policies. We prioritize building lasting relationships based on trust, integrity, and exceptional customer service.

Our mission is simple: to protect what matters most to you. Whether you are securing your family's future, providing top-tier benefits to your employees, protecting your assets, or ensuring your business is fully covered, Shea Insurance Group is here to guide you through every step of the process. With access to top-rated insurance carriers, we offer competitive rates and comprehensive coverage options, ensuring you have peace of mind when it matters most.

At Shea Insurance Group, we're more than just an insurance agency – we're a partner in safeguarding your future. Let us help you navigate the complexities of insurance with confidence and ease.

An Independent Advantage

We are Independent Agents in Wayne, Illinois, free to choose the best carrier for your insurance needs. We do not work for an insurance company; we work for you. We work on your side when you have a loss and follow through to see that you get fair, prompt payment and service. Shea Insurance Group, LLC represents a carefully selected group of financially strong, reputable insurance companies. Therefore, we are able to offer you the best coverage at the most competitive price.

What is an Independent Insurance Agent?

Consider this: You need insurance to drive a car, to purchase a house, to protect your family's financial future and to run a small business. But if there was only one insurance company that offered only one type of insurance, you wouldn't have a choice. The only solution would be to use that one company.

With an independent insurance agent, you have choices. Independent agents are not tied to any one insurance company. An independent agent works solely to satisfy your needs. They have several companies that he or she can approach to get you the best coverage at the best price. You are using an expert for an important financial decision.

When you buy insurance, you want an advocate who will properly assess your risks and give you an objective analysis of the marketplace. That's us. We give you the facts and expert advice based on years of experience and up-to-the-minute knowledge of the market. It's up to you to make the final choice.

www.ingramcontent.com/pod-product-compliance
Lightning Source LLC
LaVergne TN
LVHW051839080426
835512LV00018B/2976